Expressive Order
Confirming Sentiments in Social Actions

David R. Heise

Expressive Order

Confirming Sentiments in Social Actions

 Springer

David R. Heise
Department of Sociology
Indiana University
Bloomington, IN 47405
USA
heise@indiana.edu

Library of Congress Control Number: 2006933298

ISBN-10: 0-387-38177-5   e-ISBN-10: 0-387-38179-1
ISBN-13: 978-0-387-38177-0   e-ISBN-13: 978-0-387-38179-4

Printed on acid-free paper.

9 8 7 6 5 4 3 2 1

springer.com

To my dear wife, Elsa Lewis.

Preface

My first goal for this book is to provide a lasting sourcebook for researchers and scholars working with affect control theory. My second goal is to provide an accessible introduction to affect control theory for advanced undergraduates and graduate students. The book addresses these two very different goals with an unusual structure.

Part 1 communicates affect control theory conversationally, in words enriched with some figures and tables. The informal presentation foregoes scholarly exegeses and empirical data analyses, in favor of declarative statements of the theory's arguments, with everyday examples. A wide range of readers—including undergraduates in and out of the social sciences—should find the verbal presentation intelligible.

Part 2 presents the theory again, this time as a formal model. The mathematical formulation progresses step by step, from assumptions to derived propositions. Comprehension of the model is enhanced by a chapter that presents numerical examples and a chapter that discusses programming of the computer simulation program that implements the model. This formalization of the theory provides a level of definiteness and precision exceptional in sociology, allowing scholars and researchers in the social sciences to gain understanding of the theory's assumptions and propositions.

Part 3 of the book provides some resources for those interested in working with the theory—an overview of the theory's development and specialties, a description of the computer simulation program that can be used to design studies, and a glossary of terms.

Herman Smith read a draft of Part 1 and offered many useful suggestions, for which I am grateful. I also thank Lynn Smith-Lovin, Dawn Robinson, Neil MacKinnon, and Linda Francis for providing information used in Part 3.

David R. Heise

Contents

Part 1

Affect Control Theory, Plainly Told

1

Introduction

> By entering a situation in which he is given a face to maintain, a person takes on the responsibility of standing guard over the flow of events as they pass before him. He must ensure that a particular expressive order is sustained—an order that regulates the flow of events, large or small, so that anything that appears to be expressed by them will be consistent with his face. (Goffman 1967, p. 9)

The title of this book derives from the above statement by sociologist Erving Goffman. The theory presented in this book—affect control theory—incorporates Goffman's insight that expressive order infuses social interactions as individuals maintain their identities, or faces.

1.1 Affect Control Theory

Here's the essence of affect control theory.
- You (and every individual) create events to confirm the sentiments that you have about the identities of yourself and others in the current situation.
- Your emotions reflect your sentiment about yourself and the kinds of validations or invalidations that you are experiencing at the moment.
- If your actions don't work to maintain your sentiments, then you re-conceptualize the identities of others or yourself.
- Confirming sentiments about your current identity actualizes your sense of self, or else produces inauthenticity that you resolve by enacting compensating identities.

- In the process of building events to confirm your sentiments, you perform social roles that operate the basic institutions of society.

This overview is too brief to cover all important matters. However, chapters in this book expand the key ideas.

1.2 Utility of the Theory

Affect control theory addresses questions like these:

- What are the expected behaviors of American middle-class mothers, fathers, daughters, and sons? How do expectations vary as a result of unusual events?
- What behavior is expected of employers and employees by females and by males? Of health-care practitioners and patients? Of teachers and students? Of citizens and legal officials?
- What are typical emotional reactions to victimization—to being cheated, robbed, assaulted, molested? Do emotions differ by settings, by the identity of the victimizer, by events that occurred previously? How are others likely to view a victim when they find out about the incident?
- In a particular social situation, what does one have to do in order to feel joy or pride or calmness? What kinds of events in the situation make one feel nervous or angry or depressed?
- How might employer-employee social interaction differ in Japan and America? What would be different in the behavior and emotions of a Canadian wife interacting with a Canadian husband, as opposed to husbands and wives in the U.S.A., or in Germany?

Affect control theory provides specific answers to such questions. Many of the theory's predictions have been validated in empirical studies.

Some published statements by sociologists have recognized affect control theory's usefulness.

> Undoubtedly this is the best developed empirically applicable cybernetic model in the history of theoretical sociology. (Thomas Fararo 1989, pp. 167)

> [ACT is] the most methodologically rigorous program [in the sociology of emotions]. ... It can formulate both emotional outcomes of situations and situational outcomes of emotions in a manner that is more efficient than any other presently available in either sociology or psychology. (T. David Kemper 1991, pp. 342-3)

> [Affect control theory] offers a rigorous methodology for modeling emotion in interaction .... The models and predictions can be applied to human-computer interaction leading to the design of "socially intelligent" systems that optimize user experience and outcomes. (Lisa Troyer 2004, p. 30)

1.3 Overview of the Book

Chapters in Part I are written in a conversational style unburdened with technical details and without embedded citations to published research. These chapters present the theory in its entirety.

Chapters 2 through 4 introduce the notion of culturally-grounded sentiments varying along three dimensions of affective meaning. Such sentiments are building blocks of social experience, according to affect control theory.

Chapters 5 through 7 consider how participants define social situations and create actions to fit the situation they have defined. The focus is on affective processes of impression formation and confirmation of sentiments. However, the chapters also describe how social institutions constrain the construction of situations and actions, and how social institutions are embodied and operated by individuals as they work to maintain meanings.

Chapter 8 introduces affect control theory's approach to emotions. Attention is given to how emotions relate to motives, and to how emotions relate to stress.

Chapter 9 focuses on individuals' accommodation to realities that violate their expectations. Three general processes are considered: labeling people with new identities, making attributions about an individual's character or mood, and changing one's own sentiments.

Chapter 10 considers individuals' personal identities—their selves—and how sentiments attached to selves generate preferences for enacting some identities rather than others.

Chapters in Part II of this book present affect control theory's mathematical model. These chapters clarify what's assumed, what's empirically measured, and what's derived in the theory.

Chapter 11 propounds that the likelihood of an event can be specified in terms of pre-event sentiments and feelings about event elements. Chapters 12 and 13 use this understanding to derive solutions for optimal behaviors and for optimal identities.

Chapter 14 describes how modifiers amalgamate with identities. The amalgamation equations are solved to specify which emotions and attributions are appropriate in given circumstances.

Chapter 15 links moods with optimal identities, specifying how a person's observed emotionality may influence labeling of that individual.

Chapter 16 formalizes notions of how an individual's self-sentiment is linked to the individual's identity preferences.

Chapter 17 simplifies the mathematics presented in prior chapters in order to illustrate the kinds of calculations that are involved in the formal model, and in order to show some properties of the solutions. Chapter 18 explicates the mathematical model in a different way, by sketching how it is implemented in a computer program for simulating social interaction.

Chapters in Part III of this book review research related to affect control theory and introduce the computer simulation program that is used in research.

Chapter 19 outlines the history of the research program, and shows how the scores of publications related to affect control theory partition into a number of different areas.

Chapter 20 outlines the use of affect control theory's computer program, *Interact*. The program is important for exploring new topics and for designing empirical studies.

Appendix A provides a glossary of basic concepts in affect control theory.

1.4 Further Readings

Erving Goffman provided readable discussions of several topics of concern in affect control theory in the following books: *Presentation of Self in Everyday Life* (1959); *Asylums* (1961); *Stigma: Notes on the Management of Spoiled Identity* (1963); *Interaction Ritual: Essays on Face-to-Face Behavior* (1967).

Three previous books on affect control theory—by myself (Heise 1979); by Lynn Smith-Lovin and myself (Smith-Lovin and Heise 1988); and by Neil MacKinnon (1994)—provide details regarding empirical research on affect control theory, and regarding the relation of affect control theory to other theories.

2

Sentiments

If you are like many Americans, you feel that doctors are helpful, powerful, and reserved. That's your sentiment about doctors, the way you feel in general about them even though you might have different feelings in particular circumstances.

For many Americans, the general sentiment about children is quite different: children are good, weak, and noisy. Gangsters provoke still another sentiment: bad, powerful, and active.

2.1 Evaluation, Potency, and Activity (EPA)

Sentiments have three aspects. Evaluation concerns goodness versus badness, Potency concerns powerfulness versus powerlessness, and Activity concerns liveliness versus quietness. The three aspects are abbreviated EPA.

Each aspect, or dimension, of sentiments can be characterized by a variety of contrasts.

Some words characterizing the positive side of the Evaluation dimension are: nice, sweet, heavenly, good, mild, happy, fine, clean. Corresponding words for the negative side are: awful, sour, hellish, bad, harsh, sad, course, dirty.

Characterizations of the positive side of the Potency dimension include: big, powerful, deep, strong, high, long, full, many. The corresponding words for the negative side are: little, powerless, shallow, weak, low, short, empty, few.

Words characterizing the positive side of the Activity dimension include: fast, noisy, young, alive, known, burning, active, light. Corresponding negative words are: slow, quiet, old, dead, unknown, freezing, inactive, dark.

Characterizations within each dimension are correlated. For example, something judged sweet is likely to be judged clean also.

Characterizations across dimensions are uncorrelated. For example, sensing that something is powerful provides no clue as to whether it is good or bad.

Table 2-1. Example identities and behaviors having various configurations of evaluation, potency and activity (EPA)

EPA Configuration	Identities	Behaviors
Good, Potent, Active	champion, friend, lover	entertain, surprise, make love to
Good, Potent, Inactive	grandparent, priest, scientist	pray for, massage, console
Good, Impotent, Active	baby, child, youngster	ask about something, beckon to
Good, Impotent, Inactive	old-timer, patient, librarian	obey, observe, follow
Bad, Potent, Active	devil, bully, gangster	slay, rape, beat up
Bad, Potent, Inactive	executioner, scrooge, disciplinarian	execute, imprison, flunk
Bad, Impotent, Active	delinquent, junkie, quack	laugh at, ridicule, pester
Bad, Impotent, Inactive	loafer, has-been, bore	submit to, beg, ignore

Various kinds of people have different positions on the EPA dimensions. Table 2-1 shows some examples of kinds of people representing each configuration of EPA. Individuals' social behaviors also vary on the EPA dimensions, and Table 2-1 also shows some examples of social behaviors representing each EPA configuration.

The three aspects of sentiments—Evaluation, Potency, and Activity—are matters of degree. Each aspect can be greater or less, in either a positive or negative direction. For example, some things are slightly good, others are quite good, still others are extremely good.

You can picture the three dimensions by imagining that sentiments are floating around the room you're in.

- Things that are very good are up near the ceiling, things that are very bad are near the floor.
- Things that are powerful are near the wall in front of you, weak things are near the wall behind you.
- Lively things are on your right, and quiet things are on your left.
- Things that are neither good nor bad, powerful nor powerless, lively nor quiet hang around the center of the room.

So to see a grandparent you glance upward to your left at the good, powerful, quiet corner. To see a child you turn your head and look up over your right shoulder at the good, powerless, lively corner. To see a gangster you look down to your right at the bad, powerful, lively corner.

Ways of acting are in the room, too. Look up in front of you to your right, and there's making love to someone. Now drop your eyes to the floor along that same corner of the room, and you see raping someone. Look down behind you on the left; there's ignoring someone. Look up, forward to your left to see consoling someone.

The room represents EPA space, where sentiments about all kinds of things float inside like stars in the cosmos. EPA space also is affective space, since it is where your feelings about things are positioned.

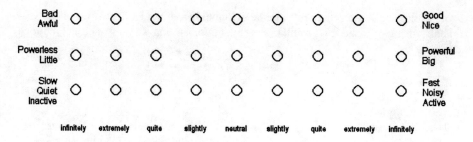

Fig. 2-1. Rating scales for measuring EPA—a "semantic differential."

2.2 Measuring EPA

You can measure your own sentiments with the three rating scales shown in Figure 2-1. Each rating scale presents adjectives at its end points in order to describe the negative and positive poles of the dimension. Nine marking positions are between the end points, and adverbs at the bottom characterize the meaning of each marking position. You indicate your feelings about something by selecting one position on each scale.

The custom is to use plus units to measure goodness, powerfulness, and liveliness; minus units for bad, powerless, or quiet. Ratings are converted into numbers depending on which position is marked.

infinitely on the left side	=	-4.3
extremely on the left side	=	-3
quite on the left side	=	-2
slightly on the left side	=	-1
neutral	=	0
slightly on the right side	=	+1
quite on the right side	=	+2
extremely on the right side	=	+3
infinitely on the right side	=	+4.3

For example, something that you rate as "quite good, nice" gets coded +2 on Evaluation.

An EPA profile is a list of three such measures: the first number represents Evaluation, the second is Potency, and the third is Activity.

Try using these scales to measure some of your own feelings about things. Write down your ratings in the form of EPA profiles.

These days, sentiments usually are measured on computer-implemented scales that let you move a pointer anywhere on the scale to reflect your feelings. Ratings in-between the choice points shown in Fig. 2-1 get coded as fractions. For example, a rating halfway between "quite" and "extremely" on the good side of the Evaluation scale would be coded +2.5.

Distances between sentiments can be computed from the EPA profiles of the sentiments, using a standard formula. For example, among some American college students:

- The average EPA profile of "enemy" is -2.1, 0.8, 0.2 among males, and -2.5, 0.6, 0.9 among females.
- The average EPA profile of "friend" is 2.8, 1.9, 1.4 among males, and 3.5, 2.5, 2.0 among females.
- The distance between enemy and friend is 5.2 for males, and 6.4 for females.
- Thus sentiments about enemy and friend are further apart for the females than for the males.

This illustrates that numerically-measured sentiments can be analyzed mathematically.

2.3 Universality of EPA

Sentiments of people everywhere vary along the three dimensions of Evaluation, Potency, and Activity. That's not just an assumption. It's an empirical finding from cross-cultural research in dozens of societies, conducted in the following steps.

1. Concepts that exist in every culture—like father, mother, child, water, moon—were assembled into a list.
2. Natives in each culture were asked to respond to each concept on the list with a modifier, and to name the opposite of that modifier. For example, some individuals in the U.S.A. might respond to mother with the word sweet, and give the word sour as the opposite.
3. The modifier opposites were formed into scales, and natives used the scales to rate each concept on the list. Ratings of a concept on a scale were averaged to get a number indicating how raters from that culture typically positioned the concept on the scale.
4. For each culture, a table was created, with a column for each scale, a row for each concept, and average ratings of concepts on scales in the cells. This allowed correlation coefficients to be computed between scales. For example, in the American table, average ratings of concepts on the sweet-sour scale and on the good-bad scale were used to compute a numerical correlation between the two scales. (Correlations near 1.0 indicate similarity; correlations near zero indicate absence of a relation; correlations near -1.0 indicate a reverse relation.)
5. A pan-cultural table also was created, allowing scales in different cultures to be correlated. For example, American average ratings of concepts on the sweet-sour scale and Mexican average ratings on a bueno-malo scale were compared across all concepts in order to define the correlation between those two scales.
6. Statistical analysis of correlations between scales showed that the scales clustered into three major groups—Evaluation, Potency, Activity—and every culture contributed scales to each group. For example, all three scales mentioned above ended up in the Evaluation cluster, indicating that con-

cepts rated as sweet by Americans tended to be rated good by Americans, and bueno by Mexicans.

In this study, the only thing translated from one language to another was the list of universal concepts. The only assumption in the analysis was that people in different cultures have roughly parallel feelings about the universal concepts, even though specific details might differ from one culture to another. (Fig. 3-1 in the next section shows that this assumption does hold cross-culturally for father, mother, and child.) Thus the cross-cultural study provides compelling evidence that sentiments around the world involve the three EPA dimensions, and the EPA dimensions are comparable in every culture.

2.4 Further Readings

Psychologist Charles Osgood with co-authors George Suci and Percy Tannenbaum (1957) instituted semantic differential rating scales in their book, *The Measurement of Meaning*. Osgood (1962) interpreted semantic differential measurements as a way of assessing affective meaning rather than meaning in general in his article, "Studies of the generality of affective meaning systems."

Osgood's book with W. May and M. Miron (1975), *Cross-Cultural Universals of Affective Meaning*, documented the massive cross-cultural project that verified the dimensions of Evaluation, Potency, and Activity as cross-cultural universals.

I reviewed early methodological work on the semantic differential (Heise 1969b). I also described techniques for obtaining EPA data over the Internet (Heise 2001).

3

Culture

While you have your own personal feelings about things, you also share sentiments with people around you. That's the notion of culture—shared meanings and feelings.

3.1 Consensus

Your sentiment about an object results in part from your private encounters with the object. Additionally your sentiment is shaped by interactions with others— individuals in your social groups, and strangers in public places or the mass media. Your encounters with others pull your sentiment toward a cultural standard.

Consider child as an example.

Your own private experiences with children are one source of your sentiment about any child. You express your sentiment in public actions toward children and in talking about children with your associates. Your public acts and comments influence others and shape their social acts. However, your associates also have private experiences with children, which they express in their public behavior and talk, thereby influencing their associates, including you. Interacting and talking together changes your sentiment toward child to be like the sentiments of your associates, and their sentiments become more like yours. A shared sentiment toward children emerges. That shared sentiment eventually affects even your private experiences with children as you try to experience children in a way that affirms the shared sentiment about them.

Observing each other's actions toward an object and talking about the object produces a norm. The existence of a sentiment norm means that individual sentiments are more similar than they would be without social process.

Norms in one group influence norms in another group when the groups are bridged by individuals who are in both groups. Virtually all groups in a society are networked together by such bridges, and thus society-wide, cultural norms form over time as normative sentiments pass back and forth between groups.

Affective intersubjectivity—a crucial aspect of social life—emerges when you are with others from the same culture as you are from. You evoke shared sentiments as you talk about your experiences, and consequently your audience feels much the same as you do about experiences that you describe to them.

3.1.1 Individuality Versus Norms

Your sentiment about an object reflects your unique experiences with the object and also reflects cultural norms. Which has the bigger impact on your sentiments—unique experiences, or cultural norms? Among individuals who are well integrated into their culture, the relative impacts are as follows.

Cultural norms dominate evaluations. Eighty percent of the variation in an individual's evaluations of things relates to norms, and just 20 percent of the variation corresponds to the individual's unique experiences.

Cultural norms influence the Potency and Activity aspects of sentiments less, but still are more important than unique experiences. On both of these dimensions, approximately 60 percent of an individual's variation in feelings relates to norms, and about 40 percent of the variation relates to unique experiences.

Thus your sentiments are predominately cultural. Your feelings about most things are very similar to the feelings of other individuals in your society.

3.1.2 Measurement Implications

An important consequence of cultural consensus is that we can measure sentiments efficiently.

Here's an example illustrating the logic.

Suppose that we take a random sample of four to find out the average height to the nearest inch of 100 humans—including three infants and 43 children—where the population mean is 4 feet. A first random sample estimates the average height as 4 feet 6 inches. However, another random sample estimates the average height as 3 feet 3 inches. Obviously, estimating the average height of the population from a sample of four can be quite misleading about the true average. To estimate the average height confidently, we need to use a much larger sample, or take a census of the whole population.

Now consider a different population of adults in which every individual is 5 feet 9 inches in height, with the population mean being 5 feet 9 inches.. (You might imagine this population consists of 100 biological clones.) A first random sample of four yields a mean of 5 feet 9 inches. A second random sample of four also has a mean of 5 feet 9 inches. Every sample of four will have a mean of 5 feet 9 inches. In fact, a sample of four is extravagant in this case. We confidently can estimate the average height of the homogeneous population from a single individual.

Socially sharing a sentiment makes individuals homogeneous with regard to the sentiment. If a group were perfectly homogeneous, then any individual would represent the group with regard to the sentiment. In partially homogeneous groups we need to average the sentiments of a few individuals to get rid of effects of unique private experiences. Yet, because of the homogeneity, all of the individual sentiments are close to the average value, and a small sample provides a good basis for assessing the cultural sentiment. Costly large-sample surveys or censuses are not required.

3.2 Cultural Stability

Cultural sentiments can change, but changes evolve gradually, even in modern societies that are pervaded with social movements, fashions, and mass media.

One way of assessing the amount of stability in cultural sentiments is to determine how well earlier sentiments predict later sentiments. Correlations near 1.0 indicate stability in sentiments. Correlations near zero indicate that sentiments change randomly from year to year.

Evaluations are very stable, with correlations of 0.90 or more, even when 25 years separate earlier and later measures. Changes in evaluation usually involve increasing or decreasing levels of goodness or of badness; switches between approval and condemnation of a concept occur infrequently. When switches in evaluation do occur, they often relate to an issue that has been the focus of recognized social change in the society. For example, identities relating to homosexuality went from condemnation to approval at the end of the 20th Century, in both Canada and the U.S.A., possibly as a consequence of the gay rights movement.

Potency assessments also are stable, though not as stable as evaluations. Correlations between potency measurements 15 to 25 years apart range between 0.80 and 0.90 in different studies. Correlations are lower for behavior potencies because behavior potencies vary only from powerful to neither powerful nor powerless, whereas other kinds of concepts have both powerful and powerless instances. Concepts rarely switch between powerfulness and powerlessness. However, an example of such switching was provided by identities of young females in the U.S.A. going from powerless to somewhat powerful at the end of the 20th Century.

Activity connotations can change more rapidly than other aspects of sentiments, with correlations ranging from 0.60 to 0.90 in different studies. For example, in the U.S.A. in the last quarter of the 20th Century activities changed substantially, with concepts relating to authority and leadership gaining in activity, and concepts concerned with deviance and withdrawal losing activity.

Most cultural sentiments remain nearly the same for decades. Moreover, some changes that do occur are temporary, lasting only a few years before the old sentiments prevail again.

You may find this hard to believe with mass media always reporting how times are changing, and when you yourself have to strive to keep your attitudes up-to-date. However, here's a whimsical allegory to illustrate how very little change can seem massive. A carousel with its bright colors, flashing lights, loud music, bobbing ponies, and circular motion is fascinating and challenging to a four-year-old. Yet basi-

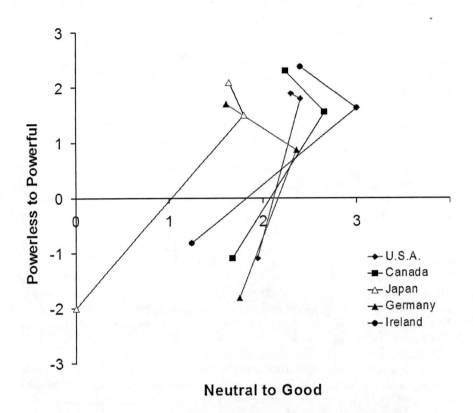

Fig. 3-1. Female sentiments about father, mother, and child in five cultures. Child is the lowest point on each line, mother is the middle point.

cally nothing is happening, so the same carousel is boring and insultingly simplistic to an eight-year-old.

We are like a four-year-old in confronting our contemporary culture. With hundreds of thousands of concepts and sentiments in the culture, a change of just one-tenth of a percent per year confronts us with hundreds of points of flux—a fascinating and challenging torrent of change. Yet the overall culture is nearly static!

3.2.1 Instability or Unreliability?

Imperfect correlations between measures of sentiments at two different times can arise from instabilities, but also from measurement errors—correlations are pulled toward zero if measurements are imprecise. Errors do occur in measuring sentiments, because of raters' fallibilities, like clumsiness in marking the rating scales, confusion in translating subjective feelings to scale positions, or temporary states of mind in which raters misconceive their own sentiments.

In fact, about a third of the variation in an individual's evaluation ratings is error, and approximately half of the variation in potency and activity ratings is error. Because of this inaccuracy, ratings of sentiments by one individual on one occasion rarely are used for anything. Instead, multiple ratings are obtained and averaged in order to offset errors in one measurement with errors from another measurement, thereby revealing the regularities that underlie the set of measurements.

Sentiment norms typically are estimated from samples of 30 or more raters. With this many raters, only about three percent of the variation in mean ratings is error in the case of evaluation, eight percent in the case of potency, and nine percent in the case of activity. Put differently, with ratings averaged over 30 raters, the maximum over-time correlation of evaluation means is about 0.97, the maximum over-time correlation of mean potency ratings is 0.92, and the maximum over-time correlation of mean activity ratings is 0.91.

Thus, some of the decrements from 1.0 in over-time sentiment correlations are due to measurement errors rather than cultural instability, and the stability correlations would be higher if corrected for the effects of measurement errors. That fact, however, only reinforces the main conclusion, that cultural sentiments are very stable.

3.3 Variations Across Cultures

Sharing sentiments with others in your society is one aspect of culture. Another aspect is having different sentiments than people in other societies.

Fig. 3-1 shows cultural sentiments for father, mother, and child as measured among people in the U.S.A., Canada, Japan, Germany, and Northern Ireland. This chart is based on female sentiments, but it would look about the same were male measurements used instead.

You can see that people in all five cultures agree that fathers, mothers, and children are not bad, and they agree that parents are powerful and children are powerless. Thus, the general structure of sentiments about nuclear family identities is parallel across societies. However, aside from this shared general structure, major differences arise among raters from different countries.

- The Japanese raters evaluate family members less positively than individuals in the other cultures; among the Japanese the average rating of child is neither good nor bad.
- Generally, parents are evaluated more positively than children, but not among the German raters who feel that fathers are less good than either children or mothers.
- Mothers generally are felt to be nicer than fathers, but this difference is negligible for the American raters. The power difference between fathers and mothers also is negligible for the Americans.

These results typify cross-cultural variations in sentiments. People in different cultures share some general perspectives, yet specific sentiments vary from one culture to another.

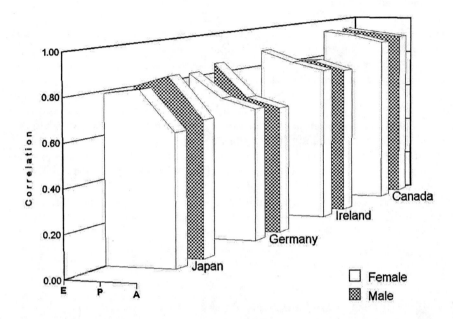

Fig. 3-2. Correlations of American identity sentiments with identity sentiments in four other nations.

Correlation analysis provides a way to assess the degree of cross-cultural sharing. You compute a correlation coefficient to see how well you can predict sentiments in one culture from sentiments in another culture. The graph in Fig. 3-2 shows how accurately other cultures' EPA sentiments about identities can be predicted from U.S.A. values.

To illustrate, the front-most bar shows that Japanese females' evaluation ratings of identities can be predicted well from evaluation ratings of identities by females in the U.S.A., the correlation coefficient being almost 0.8. Evaluation ratings of identities also are quite parallel among Japanese males and American males. Potency ratings of identities by Japanese and Americans correlate somewhat higher than evaluation ratings, for both females and males. However, Japanese activity ratings of identities and U.S.A. activity ratings correlate less, around 0.65 for females, and 0.70 for males.

Overall, Fig. 3-2 shows that all of the cultures share general perspectives with the U.S.A., in that all of the correlations are substantially positive. Yet patterns in other cultures vary at least a little from U.S.A. patterns, in that none of the correlations reaches 1.0. The U.S.A. and Canada are most similar. Identity sentiments in other cultures diverge further from U.S.A. sentiments.

In the case of behaviors, U.S.A. evaluation ratings predict evaluation ratings in other cultures well (with all correlations above 0.86, for both females and males). U.S.A. potency ratings of behaviors have a relatively low correspondence with potency ratings in other cultures (with correlations ranging from 0.38 to 0.60). U.S.A. activity ratings of behaviors correlate with corresponding ratings in Canada, Germany, and Japan (with correlations between 0.67 and 0.81), but less so with ratings in Ireland (0.43 for females, 0.50 for males).

Studying numerous graphs like these reveals that evaluations are remarkably similar in these five societies, with a mean cross-culture correlation coefficient of 0.81 for social identities and 0.88 for behaviors. So people brought up in these Asian, European, and North American cultures largely agree about who is good and who is bad, and about which actions are moral and which are immoral.

Notions of who is relatively powerful and who is relatively powerless also are similar across societies. Cross-cultural consensus drops dramatically in judgments regarding the potencies of behaviors. However, almost all behavior potencies are positive rather than both positive and negative, and correlations generally decline with a reduced range of variation.

Feelings about the relative activity or passivity of identities and of behaviors are substantially shared across the cultures.

In conclusion, the results reveal a substantial international correspondence in the allocation of honor and stigma, and of power and dependency, to different kinds of people. A substantial international concordance also prevails regarding the morality of behaviors. Feelings about the relative power of different kinds of behaviors are somewhat shared cross-culturally, but correlations are lower in this case than in other comparisons. Substantial cross-cultural similitude characterizes feelings about the relative activation of kinds of people and of kinds of behaviors.

3.4 Further Readings

The notion of culture as consensus has been developed rigorously by A. Kimball Romney, S. C. Weller, and William H. Batchelder in "Culture as consensus: A theory of culture and informant accuracy" (1986); and "Recent applications of cultural consensus theory" (1987).

The flow of influence within a population was analyzed by Noah Friedkin in his 1998 book, *A Structural Theory of Social Influence*, and in an article with Eugene C. Johnsen (2003).

My 2001 article, "Project Magellan: Collecting Cross-Cultural Affective Meanings Via the Internet," presents cross-cultural comparisons of sentiments about identities and behaviors in more detail.

Neil MacKinnon and Alison Luke (2002) studied over-time changes in Canadian sentiments. My estimates of sentiment stability are derived in a methodological study of semantic differentials, *Measuring Sentiments*, which will be published as a book.

4

Sub-Cultures

Are you in a clique or community that is separate from the mainstream—a group that is involved in an unorthodox religion, an offbeat sexual preference, an oddball entertainment? If so, then ...

- You share most of your sentiments with other people in your society. Being in a special group doesn't give you a different culture.
- You do differ in sentiments for concepts that are most relevant to your unique membership.

Individuals who disagree too much to adopt a society's normative sentiment about something may gravitate to a special group that provides them with better affective resonance. As individuals segregate themselves in this way, diverging pockets of consensus—or subcultures—emerge. Societal diversity in sentiments about an issue often corresponds not to anarchic individuality but to the existence of sub-cultures.

A sub-culture consists of special meanings maintained within a sub-population of a society. Any aggregate of people who segregate some of their interactions may develop a sub-culture.

Sub-cultures orbit around types of people, actions, and material objects that are of special significance within the sub-population. Individuals in the sub-population typically have more positive sentiments about the focal matters than do individuals in the culture at large. For example, drug users maintain a sub-culture in which drug users, drug experiences, and drug paraphernalia are more positively evaluated than in the general culture.

Here are illustrations.

4.1 Gender

Do the feelings you have in social interaction differ from feelings experienced by the opposite sex? In the U.S.A. the answer is yes. Females and males have different sentiments about certain things, though not about a lot of things.

One U.S.A. study statistically tested male EPA ratings against females' ratings to see if they were different. The study found differences, but only barely beyond what would be expected by chance. Twelve percent of the male and female sentiments differed on Evaluation, Potency, or Activity to some degree, whereas ten percent would be expected by chance.

The key difference between female and male sentiments is that males are less condemning than females of sexuality identities, behaviors, and settings. For example, males give less negative ratings than females to the identities of bisexual, heterosexual, hooker, peeping tom, call girl, mistress, or porno star; to the behaviors of seduce, deflower, disrobe, undress, ravish, or rape; and to the settings of bedroom, burlesque show, topless bar, or orgy. Such male-female differences in evaluations of sexuality also appear in Canada, Germany, Japan, and China, so a gender difference in evaluating sexuality is a safe generalization.

4.1.1 A Pseudo-Sub-Culture

Aside from the difference in sentiments about sexuality, gender provides a case of a pseudo-sub-culture. That is, females and males sometimes differ in feelings and actions, not because they have different sentiments, but because they occupy discrete identities associated with different sentiments. More potency may be attributed to male identities than to the female counterparts.

In the following list, the first-named identity in each gendered pair was the identity with more potency according to a study in the U.S.A. during the 1970s.

> son-daughter, brother-sister, *nephew-niece*, *grandson-granddaughter*, boy-girl, man-woman, *husband-wife*, grandfather-grandmother, hero-heroine, *landlord-landlady*, adulterer-adulteress, *mother-father*

Male identities were more potent in all pairs except mother-father. Even the mother-father pair was not much of an exception since mother and father were nearly the same in powerfulness.

The relative powerlessness of female identities did not come from male chauvinism of the raters, since the ratings of potency in this analysis came solely from females!

The potency advantage for male identities in 20th Century America is no quirk of American culture. The same pattern in sentiments occurred for German females, too. Even for females in the People's Republic of China, male identities were more potent than female identities, despite a half century of radical communist leadership committed to raising the status of women in China!

On the other hand, the pattern appears to be dissipating in America. A 1990s study in the U.S.A. shows some deviations from this pattern with woman and wife being at least as powerful as the male counterparts. In data collected early in the 21st Century, U.S.A. females were rating a number of female identities higher in potency than the corresponding male identities—all of the instances italicized in the list above. This suggests that the potency of female identities is increasing in the U.S.A., perhaps as a result of the feminist social movement.

4.1.2 Gendered Traits

According to a study done with Canadian and U.S.A. data, personality traits that imply a person is "productive, accomplished, and up for any type of challenge" typically are viewed as male, whereas the opposite kinds of traits are female. Thus stereotypical male traits include active, confident, energetic, adventurous, stable, strong, industrious, wise, an independent. Stereotypical female traits include foolish, inhibited, snobbish, unstable, unambitious, and weak.

However, among traits with moderate potency another gender distinction arises: the positively evaluated traits seem characteristic of women, and the negatively evaluated traits seem characteristic of men. So stereotypical male traits also include cruel, hostile, tough, and self-centered; whereas stereotypical female traits include sentimental, gentle, emotional, kind, sincere, and helpful. In this case, females seem nice in that they care about others, whereas men seem nasty in that they just look out for themselves.

One way of summarizing the results is that stereotypical traits give men a power advantage, and give women a status advantage. Men can get others to please them by setting up punishment-reward contingencies. Women, on the other hand, having the kind of status that derives from others' esteem, may have others pleasing them without instigation.

4.2 Gay Christians

Members of a gay fundamentalist church congregation in 1970s South Carolina saw the identities of Christian and homosexual more positively than did most Americans at the time. In particular, the goodness and powerfulness that the gay Christians associated with the identity of homosexual was opposite from others' feelings.

A method of analysis described in Part 3 of this book—the *Interact* simulation program—allows us to conjecture that the gay homosexuals' sentiments would have generated friendly, supportive interactions between gays and Christians. Such interactions theoretically included behaviors like greet, welcome, entertain, amuse, encourage, or compliment; and emotional states like compassionate, pleased, generous, touched, moved, contented, or charmed. Thus sentiments within the gay sub-culture theoretically permitted gays to behave normally and view themselves as positive interaction partners.

On the other hand, members of a southern Unitarian church in the 1970s rated Christian positively (though not as positively as the fundamentalist church members) and homosexual negatively. The negative evaluation of homosexual typified the general culture at that time. Theoretically, those sentiments would have produced interactions between gays and Christians that were not very satisfying for either party. The homosexual's behaviors might have included tease, deride, annoy, needle, heckle, or blame; while the Christian's behaviors might have included examine, query, discipline, or analyze. The homosexual's emotions during the interaction could have included both anxiety and lightheartedness; the Christian's emotions would have included self-consciousness, apprehension, shock, or nervousness. Thus, homosexuals would have had to behave deviantly and produce few pleasant emotions for others if they accepted the sentiment about gays prevailing in the general culture.

A later survey of the two church congregations revealed that the Unitarians actually did have the expectations theoretically deduced from their sentiments, and the gay Christians saw their interactions in the positive manner generated from their positive sentiments.

4.3 Deviance Sub-Cultures

The negative sentiments we have about deviants allow us to predict deviants' behavior—on the whole, we expect bad people to behave badly, which they often do. Moreover, imagining that deviants share our negative sentiments about them allows us to understand their motives as well—bad people are driven to exercise their villainy, which makes them engage in malicious acts.

By stigmatizing deviants we make their conduct comprehensible, and that is so useful that we rarely question whether deviants have the same interpretations as we do. We imagine that they must because they engage in the very actions that confirm their stigma!

Yet lay intuitions about deviant psychology sometimes are wrong. Deviants in sub-cultures acquire positive sentiments about the sub-culture's special identities and actions. Then those identities elicit the characteristic behaviors of the deviants, not because the identities and behaviors are bad, but because they are good! That is, subcultural deviants do not feel they are engaging in despicable actions. They define themselves and their actions as positive.

Fig. 4-1 makes the point vividly. The chart is based on self-reports given anonymously in 1980s deviance classes at a large American university, and it shows how 94 females and 62 males evaluated "smoking marijuana, hash" and "sniffing cocaine," depending on their total experience with recreational drugs. The center of a circle shows the average ratings of the two drugs within the group represented by the circle. The diameters of the circles show the percentages of respondents in the different groups, by sex.

You can see that people who had no experience with recreational drugs viewed both kinds of drug use as wicked. Those who tried marijuana but nothing else viewed sniffing cocaine less negatively than non-users, and they felt that smoking marijuana is neither bad nor good. Those who tried both marijuana and cocaine felt that using these drugs is a positive act. And those far enough into the drug sub-culture to have tried LSD as well as the other two drugs not only felt positive about drug usage, they felt that using marijuana is quite good!

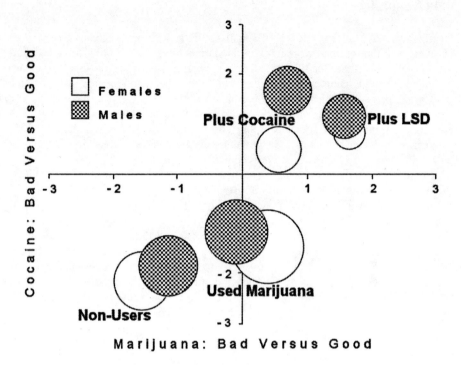

Fig. 4-1. Average evaluations of marijuana and cocaine among females and males who have used or not used marijuana, cocaine, and LSD. Circle size shows percentage of respondents at each level of drug experience.

The same finding replicates again and again in self-report studies. For example, those with experience in occult sub-cultures view invoking spirits positively, in contrast to others' views that this is devilish or farcical. Students who have threatened someone with a weapon see this as positive, self-reassuring behavior in contrast to the abhorrence expressed by others. Students with sado-masochistic sexual experience see such acts positively in contrast to the general condemnatory view.

4.3.1 Non-Normalized Deviants

Not all deviants normalize their identities or behaviors. Some really act out the plots we provide for them as deviants. They are the ones we might identify as psychiatrically disturbed in the sense that they maintain negative self-sentiments, confirm their negative self-concepts through behaviors that they believe are bad, and endure the capricious and frequently negative emotions that such behavior induces.

More on that later!

4.4 Occupations

Occupations have different levels of social standing, with professionals like doctors and judges at the top, and workers who do simple and subservient work—like boot-blacks—at the bottom. Position in the occupational hierarchy relates to average education and average income. Occupations with high social standing are those in which most of the people pursuing that occupation are well educated and well paid.

Sentiments associated with occupations reflect social standing somewhat. The education component of social standing corresponds roughly to evaluation of the occupation, at least for occupations where not everyone has a college degree. Income corresponds roughly to the occupation's potency.

Nearly every occupation has a sub-culture, at least to the extent of workers within the occupation evaluating their job more positively than do outsiders. Members of the occupation also may develop special sentiments regarding particular kinds of people and objects that they encounter frequently.

For example, a study of state police officers found that the troopers attributed more goodness, potency, and activity to themselves than college students attributed to them. Additionally, the troopers felt criminals are substantially less bad and less weak than suggested by student sentiments about criminals. Their special sentiments relate to the fact that troopers interact in a competitive, non-aggressive way with criminals, as required in their role, rather than in a conflictual, melodramatic way that would correspond with public sentiments about troopers and criminals.

4.5 Further Readings

I reported differences between male and female sentiments in the appendix of my book, *Understanding Events* (Heise 1979). Tom Langford and Neil MacKinnon (2000) reported their research on gendered traits in their article "The affective basis for the gendering of traits: Comparing the United States and Canada."

Lynn Smith-Lovin and William Douglass described their studies of gay and non-gay Christians in their 1992 article "An affect-control analysis of two religious groups."

MacKinnon and Langford assessed the relation between EPA and the average income and education of occupations in their 1994 article, "The meaning of occupational prestige scores: A social psychological analysis and interpretation." I reported the study of state troopers in Chapter 4 of *Understanding Events* (Heise 1979).

5

Defining Situations

When you enter a place, you figure out who you and others are so that you know how to act. Usually you define the situation fast and unconsciously because others' identities are evident from their uniforms (like a bus-driver) or you're encountering someone who always has the same role with you (like your mother). But the complexities of defining a situation become evident when an expected situation vanishes.

You probably have walked into a room expecting one group of people—like co-workers—and found someone else instead—like your sweetheart. When such a thing happens you are forced to re-define the situation. You can feel yourself dropping the readiness for some actions and preparing yourself to act in other ways.

Who you are depends on who others are, and what roles others take depend on the role you have. Thus you have to figure out these problems simultaneously. The solution to the puzzle of defining everyone may require more information, like knowing where you are. You and a co-worker aren't supposed to act like sweethearts at the place you work; and it's strange to act like co-workers when you and your sweetheart are alone in a cozy romantic restaurant.

5.1 Identities

Colloquial English has about 10,000 identities that can be assigned to people in everyday situations. About two-fifths of these relate to occupations and socioeconomic status, suggesting that work and wealth are preeminent factors in defining many social situations. Another ten percent of the identities manifest aspects of kinship, politics, or religion. Thus about half of the available identities available for defining social situations relate to basic social institutions of society.

About one eighth of the identities are linked to an individual's body in one way or another. This includes identities tied to an individual's sex or age—e.g., school-girl, altar-boy, heroine, womanizer, gent, lady, crone, or geezer—as well as some of the kinship identities, like sister and nephew. Also in this category are specific racial labels, like white-trash, half-breed, or black. Some identities in this category link to specific body features, like runt, brunette, and mute.

Ethnic labels identifying an individual's ancestral heritage (excluding race) or geographic station constitute another five percent of identities. Examples include Italian, Hopi, Cockney, and Hoosier.

About ten percent of common identities lay an evaluative judgment on the individual who has the identity. Most of these stigmatize—e.g., bore, grouch, snob, scum-bag, bully, dimwit, patsy, oaf, sissy, or jerk. A few of the evaluative identities enfold a person with esteem, such as boyfriend, buddy, humanitarian, square-shooter, or self-starter.

About five percent of identities relate to avocations and leisure pursuits. Some examples are baseball-player, goalie, mountaineer, scuba-diver, tourist, hiker, moviegoer, coin-collector, or smoker. Another one percent relates to sexual activities—e.g., straight, bisexual, lesbian, libertine, or pervert.

No individual qualifies for all 10,000 identities. For example, just among occupations an individual would rarely be able to claim more than one of the following: coal-miner, lumberjack, dental hygienist, bailiff, assessor, senator, landscape-architect, banker, and private-detective. However, most adults in contemporary society have hundreds of identities that they may adopt —between 500 and 1,000.

You yourself probably have seven or eight hundred identities to choose from in a new social situation. So do most others who are in the situation with you. Thus, defining a situation can be an intellectual challenge.

5.2 Institutions

Social institutions are constellations of identities, settings, and actions relating to some elementary concern. They organize the huge number of identities that you can encounter, greatly simplifying the definition of situations. Figure out which institution's cues predominate at a given time and place, and you can infer that everyone at the scene probably has identities associated with that institution.

For example, if you're in a hospital, in a room where some people are dressed in white, and some individuals are supervising others, then, chances are, you are in a medical situation, and the individuals who are present have identities like doctor, nurse, technician, patient. Or if you're in a church, and an individual dressed in black is sermonizing others who are seated, then you likely are in a religious situation, with individuals who can be assigned identities like pastor, choir member, deacon, parishioner.

Among the institutions that you are likely to encounter in everyday life are the following.

The **Family** institution contains three clusters. *Marriage* related actions include marrying, committing adultery, and divorcing. Identities in this cluster include bachelor, spinster, fiancée, fiancé, bride, bridegroom, honeymooner, newlywed, husband, wife, widow, widower, adulteress, adulterer, mistress, divorce lawyer, divorcée, divorcé, ex-wife, and ex-husband.

Begetting, nurturing, and raising children relate to a *care-giving* cluster of identities in the family that includes parents, grandparents, siblings, and collateral relatives, as well as in-laws, step-relations, foster-relations, and babysitter. Some stigmatized identities in this group include illegitimate child, orphan, and deadbeat dad.

Apart from care-giving, another cluster of family identities relates to the world of *children*: infant, child, daughter, son, girl, boy, schoolgirl, or schoolboy; and also adults who orient toward pre-puberty children—schoolteacher, pediatrician, homemaker, and family man. Stigmatized identities in this group include truant, child molester, and abortionist.

Matters of sexual attraction, sexual activities, and sexual pleasuring traditionally were part of the family, but legitimation of homosexuality and other sexual preferences have cleaved **Sexuality** away from the family into a separate institution. Its identities include heterosexual, intimate, flirt, pickup, lady-killer, stud, lecher, adulterer, nymphomaniac, slut, adulteress, homosexual, gay, bisexual, lesbian, dyke, swinger, voyeur, sadist, masochist, prostitute, gigolo, pimp, rapist, and gynecologist.

At least two clusters of identities populate the **Business** institution. One cluster deals with people who are *working* at a job in a business, office, organization, company, etc., and may be engaged in hiring, employing, controlling, and paying. Among the relevant identities are employer, boss, foreman, worker, employee, work mate, co-worker, skilled worker, temporary worker, apprentice, intern, instructor, and trainee. The cluster also has disvalued identities for those whose work performance is deficient—clock watcher and do-nothing—plus identities for those who are separated from the work world like retiree and unemployed person.

Another *commercial* cluster involves selling, buying, and paying for goods and services in shops, stores, restaurants, etc. The cluster includes identities for those buying—customer, shopper and purchaser—and also includes identities for those selling: saleslady, salesman, salesclerk, and merchant. Additionally there are identities for individuals who deliver purchases such as server, waitress and waiter. Shoppers who forego paying are in this cluster—shoplifter—and also sellers of sexual services—e.g., hooker, call girl, pimp, and gigolo.

Identities related to **Religion** partition into two groups. *Ecclesiastic* identities are for those who interpret religious doctrine—preacher, evangelist, and saint—or conduct religious rites: clergyman, priest, priestess, minister, pastor, or rabbi. Types of individuals in a congregation—like protestant, catholic, or born-again Christian—also are in this cluster. A *divinity* cluster includes identities of supernatural beings, such as God and devil, and identities defined by a relation to the supernatural, such as pagan, devil worshiper, atheist, or agnostic.

The **Education** institution embraces those who enroll in universities, colleges, and other schools in order to study and learn, as well as those who do the teaching and training. Among the identities of this institution are student, undergraduate, coed, grind, scholar, graduate student, teacher, professor, lecturer, alumnus, and dropout.

The **Medical** institution embraces specialists licensed to treat or to perform operations on people who are ill, injured, or hurt. Patient and invalid are identities for those receiving care. Doctor identities include physician, surgeon, psychiatrist, doctor, gynecologist, and pediatrician, as well as the negatively evaluated identities of abortionist, sawbones, shrink, and quack. The institutional identities also name kinds of nurses: e.g., registered nurse, head nurse, practical nurse.

The **Legal** institution has two clusters. A *law* component focuses on professionals who practice law—advising people on legal matters, conducting lawsuits, and speaking for clients in courts—or who represent the state and accuse people of crimes. The institutional identities include lawyer, attorney, defense attorney, divorce lawyer, and mouth-piece; plus the state officials of prosecuting attorney, district attorney, public defender, and judge. Labels for courtroom participants who are not legal professionals also are relevant identities: e.g., jury foreman and sheriff on the one hand, and felon, criminal, or crook on the other hand. A *police* component of law embraces members of police forces—such as police officer, cop, detective, state trooper, patrolman, plainclothesman, or nark. Some types of individuals who link with police in one way or another also are in the component: e.g., vigilante, stool-pigeon, or informer.

The **Political** institution has two branches. The *executive* component includes the identities of head, leader, governor, mayor, president, plus lower level office holders like assessor, auditor, recorder, treasurer, etc. The *electoral* component collects the identities of senator, politician, representative, candidate, lobbyist, legislator, conservative, alderman, and voter and citizen.

Other everyday institutions that haven't been delineated empirically yet include **Traveling** and **Entertainment**. The traveling institution presumably contains identities like driver, passenger, commuter, conductor, flight attendant, traveler. The entertainment institution encompasses identities like fan, athlete, movie-goer, movie star, host and hostess, guest.

The above institutions impinge on the lives of most individuals. Still more institutions exist in contemporary society—e.g., the **Military** and **Science**—but these organize daily experiences for comparatively few people.

Institutional identities are associated with general social roles that set expectations about what you and the other person should do in a scene. Even an intimate identity like sweetheart involves a general role defining proper behavior.

5.2.1 Cues to Institutions

You participate in various social institutions on a regularly scheduled basis during much of your life. Fig. 5-1 illustrates the idea for a hypothetical adult living in a suburb of a city. Every weekday the individual gets up early and shares some time with family members, then commutes to work in the city, stays a full work day, and commutes home for a few more hours with family. Saturday morning is spent with family, and the afternoon and evening are devoted to entertainments like socializing with friends, sports, and TV. Sunday is similar to Saturday, except some of the morning hours are devoted to religion. This weekly pattern repeats for most of the year, but for a few weeks during the individual's vacation, weekday time is committed to family, travel, and entertainment instead of to work. Time committed to specific institutions also varies at different stages in the individual's lifetime. For example, a youth is engaged with education instead of work, an elder frequently is engaged with the institution of medicine.

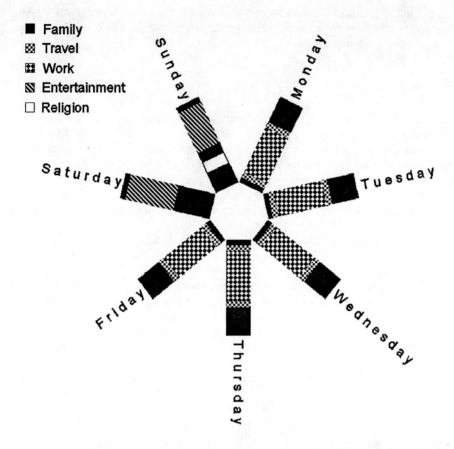

- ■ Family
- ▨ Travel
- ▦ Work
- ▨ Entertainment
- □ Religion

Fig. 5-1. Time committed to various institutions for a hypothetical individual. Mornings are at the center of the diagram, evenings are at the outer ends of the bars.

Such scheduled allocation of time to institutions is the norm for nearly everyone, even though time committed to specific institutions varies from one individual to another.

Thus, at any time you probably should be participating in some institution, and your first cue about your immediate situation is provided by your timepiece. Knowing the day and time, you know what institution you are supposed to be in—like the frazzled tourist who says, Today is Tuesday so I must be in Rome. Point of time greatly limits the likely situations you have to consider.

Your physical setting provides a second cue regarding the situation you are in. Most institutions have designated places where the institution's activities properly occur. For example, the medical institution is centered largely in ambulances, operating rooms, examination rooms, patient rooms, asylums, sanatoriums. Being in one of these places means that you probably should define the situation in terms of medical identities. Moreover, the likely identities are different in each of these places—e.g., in an ambulance, versus an operating room, versus a patient's room in a hospital—so recognizing your specific location narrows the situational possibilities down to a subset of an institution's identities.

5.3 Selves

Your self-sentiment also enters into the process of defining situations. You choose identities as a way of expressing yourself, of affirming the kind of person you are, even while fitting in with requirements of social institutions. Given a choice, you prefer social institutions that allot you identities with sentiments matching your self-sentiment. Within a given social institution, you prefer to take identities with sentiments closest to your self-sentiment. Encountering another individual, you prefer an identity that expresses your self-sentiment, and you try to cast the other into a complementary identity.

For example, suppose that you are a person with good self-esteem, thinking of yourself as capable, and also as somewhat introverted. Education, medicine, and religion are institutions providing a wealth of identities for expressing yourself. Within, say, academia, you incline toward identities like scholar, graduate student, or professor, while avoiding high-spirited academic identities like undergraduate or jock. As a student, you sometimes may cast other students into the identity of dullard, allowing you to take your preferred roles of tutor or helper with them.

Continuing the example, suppose you are the same kind of person, but extraverted instead of introverted. Now business, politics, and sexuality are institutions where you have many opportunities for self-expression. In the business world, you prefer identities like partner, negotiator, or organizer, and avoid identities like clerk or secretary. As a worker, you see co-workers as members of a team, allowing you to take your preferred role of teammate with them.

Of course, you do not always have a choice of identity. An extraverted individual with bills to pay may work as an aide, because that is the only job available, even though the aide identity does not express the individual's self well. Being somewhat inauthentic for that person, the aide identity creates a need for a compensatory identity, as discussed in Chapter 10.

5.4 Multiple Identities

You can maintain several different identities in a situation—for example, when you throw a party you may act as friend, host, and housekeeper, alternating among these identities for the performance of different kinds of behavior and to comprehend others' actions. Switching among identities as you interpret a particular event can change the self-significance of the event and compound your consequent emotions. For example, a guest who spills a glass of red wine on your carpet may have you aghast as a housekeeper, even while you display nonchalance as a host, and commiseration as a friend.

Some identities operate outside of regular institutions—for example, friendship identities, ethnic and racial identities, biological identities, mental-endeavor identities, and some stigmatizing identities. Such identities often co-occur with formal institutional identifications. For example, a man holding nearly any institutional identity simultaneously might be considered a friend, an Arab, a brunette, an expert, or a cad.

These tangential identities—sometimes called social identities as opposed to role identities—so often co-occur with other identities that they typically have a modifier form allowing them to be combined easily with identity nouns—e.g., an Arab intellectual, an intellectual Arab, ·a female golfer, an alcoholic judge. The modifier version promotes defining situations in terms of a participant's multiple identities.

5.4.1 Identity Modifiers

Sometimes you have personal information about an individual, and you qualify your definition of a situation involving the person to reflect your knowledge. You particularize the person's basic identity with specifications of traits, moods, biological characteristics, statuses, or moral dispositions. You thereby adjust general role expectations so as to better fit that particular individual..

Table 5-1. Example personality traits having various configurations of evaluation, potency and activity (EPA)

EPA Configuration	Trait
Good, Potent, Active	industrious, brave
Good, Potent, Inactive	wise, sincere
Good, Impotent, Active	carefree, impressionable
Good, Impotent, Inactive	humble, soft-spoken
Bad, Potent, Active	ruthless, belligerent
Bad, Potent, Inactive	strict, smug
Bad, Impotent, Active	rude, childish
Bad, Impotent, Inactive	lazy, withdrawn

Traits provide the most flexible means of characterizing an individual's uniqueness in a situation. Trait attribution is a way of understanding a person as more pleasant or more unpleasant than most people who perform a given role, as livelier or quieter, as more commanding or less so. Table 5-1 shows a few of the hundreds of trait names available in English.

Attributing a trait to a person amounts to assuming that the individual participates in every social situation in a special way, with role performances always skewed idiosyncratically. You are likely to attribute a trait after you note that an individual engaged in some abnormal action with regard to her or his situational identity, without repairing the impressions created by the peculiar action. Attributing a trait allows you to understand the peculiarity as being due to the individual's character or personality.

Sometimes you account for an individual's peculiar social participation by stressing a biological characteristic of the person—like sex, age, body type, disability—or a status that the person has—like wealth, education, class. Like personality traits, these adjust the expected pleasantness, liveliness, and dominance of the person's performances in a situation. Imagine a friend telling you that he left your car with an aged, fat, half-blind, illiterate, and impoverished car mechanic! You might guess that your car will end up in worse shape than it started, unless that mechanic has special genius in her fingers!

Still another way that you adjust your expectations for people is by noting the kind of characters that they have: moral, noble, helpful, kind, fair, sensible—or immoral, petty, selfish, mean, unfair, foolish. This kind of qualification is especially useful when you want to put a rhetorical handle on the person, in order to negotiate with her ("you're a fair person, right?") or with others ("she's too selfish to depend on").

Moods are still another way of characterizing an individual's uniqueness in a situation. A mood interprets a person's peculiar social participation as due to a temporary affective state, applying just in the current situation and at the present time—not in all situations, and not even in the same situation on other days. Some moods that can be attributed to someone are: calm, relaxed; happy, ecstatic; scornful, contemptuous; lonely, depressed; panicked, tormented. As you can see, moods are named with same words as emotions. However, moods are temporary aspects of an individual's identity, whereas emotions are not.

5.5 Further Readings

This chapter draws heavily on a book being written by Neil MacKinnon and myself, *Identities, Selves, and Social Institutions*, for information about kinds of identities, the institutional partitioning of identities, social identities as modifiers, and the importance of institutions and self-sentiments in defining situations. A classic work addressing some of these issues is George McCall and Jerry Simmons' 1978 book, *Identities and Interactions*. A contemporary view is provided by James Holstein and Jaber Gubrium (2000) in *The Self We Live By: Narrative Identity in a Postmodern World*.

Lynn Smith-Lovin has been exploring the topic of multiple identities and complex emotions (Smith-Lovin 2002; 2003). Modifier-identity combinations were analyzed in an article by Christine Averett and myself, "Modified social identities: Amalgamations, attributions, and emotions" (Averett and Heise, 1987), available in the book, *Analyzing Social Interaction* (Smith-Lovin and Heise, 1988).

6

Interpreting Actions

An action is a happening that you interpret as an actor doing something. Innumerable processes—like movements of galaxies—are not actions as long as no one interprets them as an actor doing something. On the other hand, some fake happenings get interpreted as real actions. Watching Hamlet hold up a skull and say, "Alas poor Yorick," you know that the actor is just pretending—that a real happening is not occurring, but you experience his speech as if he were a prince of Denmark and the skull were that of a court jester the prince once knew.

Your ability to interpret actions is built into the language you speak. Languages everywhere provide nouns and verbs that describe actions in noun-verb sentences (The child grinned) and noun-verb-noun sentences (The mother kissed the child). Your native language also may use additional nouns to specify where or when actions occur (The child played in the schoolyard), and other features of actions. The order of noun-verb combinations makes a difference when describing actions. Compare "The mother spanked the child," with "The child spanked the mother"!

Interpreting actions involves both cognitive processing and affective processing. A general rule governs both cases.

Humans try to experience what they already know.

On the cognitive side, this means that you try to fit any experience into cognitive categories acquired before the experience. The interpretation problem is figuring out which categories best fit the experience.

On the affective side, the general principle means that you try to match the feelings that the experience gives you with sentiments you acquired in the past. The interpretation problem is to choose the most sentiment-affirming interpretation among the alternatives that are available.

Clarifying terminology helps in understanding the interpretation of actions.

An *event* is any happening interpreted in terms of noun-verb combinations.

An *actor*, or agent, is an entity—like a human—that chooses to create events that fit perceived circumstances. Human actors are specified by identity-nouns.

A *behavior*, or act, describes something an actor does. Behaviors are specified by verbs.

An *object* is the target of an actor's behavior. This book deals only with objects who themselves are actors, so the objects also are specified by identity-nouns.

A *setting* is a place or time at which actions occur. Settings are specified by setting-nouns.

A *social action* is an event in which an actor behaves toward another actor who is in the role of object. The setting may or may not be mentioned when describing the action.

6.1 Action Frames

Actor, behavior, object, and setting define grammatical slots in "case grammar" of linguistic theory. A list of cultural elements specifies what can be substituted into each slot. The frame below shows the idea, with a sample of five elements that can be used in each slot. Of course, the English language actually provides hundreds of options for each slot. (Choices within square brackets show variations associated with other aspects of English grammar.)

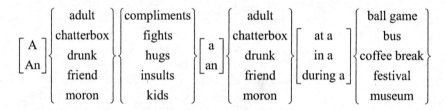

The frame implies that you interpret social actions by selecting from culturally-given lists—a noun specifying the identity of the actor, a verb specifying the behavior, a noun specifying the identity of the object, a noun specifying the setting.

Usually you interpret actions after you have defined the situation, so you already know what the setting is, and what identities the actor and object have. Then the only issue is deciding what behavior describes the actor's activity.

Specifying the behavior is partly a perceptual matter. Suppose, for instance, that you see a man turn away from a woman and exit through a doorway. Your perceptions eliminate hundreds of possible behavior specifications—e.g., you are not witnessing a case of greeting, supervising, agreeing with, collaborating with, or pursuing. Some other interpretations—such as bartering, jesting, training, or play-acting—are conceivable with the understanding that the man is feigning his behavior. A behavior that naturally fits your sequence of perceptions is departing from, and therefore you may decide that the man is departing from the woman.

6.1.1 Institutional Coherence

Not every combination of identities, behaviors, and settings makes sense. Consider, for example, this one: The judge medicated the professor during Mass. Such a social action isn't impossible, but it is so bizarre that you would resist interpreting an action in those terms!

As a general rule, proper social actions do not mix identities, behaviors, and settings from different social institutions. That's what's wrong with the medicating action. Judge is an identity in the legal institution, medicating is a behavior in the medical institution, professor is an identity in the educational institution, and Mass is a setting in the religious institution. For comparison, consider this action in which identities, behavior, and setting all are from the legal institution: The judge sentenced the defendant in the courtroom. Much more comprehensible!

6.2 Affective Processing

Cognition doesn't completely determine interpretations of behavior because perceptions often fit a number of cognitive interpretations equally well.

For example, returning to the man-leaving-woman example, the cognitive frame that befits the act of departing-from also fits additional acts: abandon, leave, desert, escape-from, or flee. How do you decide which one of these behaviors happened in the scene? Did the man leave the woman, or abandon her? Maybe he was escaping her. Perhaps he fled from her. What actually happened?

Affect resolves ambiguities left by cognitive conceptualizations. Interpretation of your experiences has to be cognitively accurate, and affectively apropos as well. After you've fitted your perceptions to your cognitions as closely as possible, you complete the process of interpretation by fitting your immediate feelings to your pre-existing sentiments as much as possible.

6.2.1 Impression-Formation

You have feelings about an actor, behavior, object, and setting when a social action begins, and new affective meanings emerge as you discern the action.

For example, suppose you observe an employer in an office cheat an employee. Based on your sentiments, you may feel positive toward the employer, employee, and office to begin with, and feel that cheating someone is reprehensible. Seeing the employer cheat the employee makes the employer seem very bad. The event neutralizes the employee, too, as if you suspect that this individual might deserve victimization. The office no longer seems a positive place, now that you know that dishonest things happen there. Even the meaning of cheating changes a bit in the context of this event: it still seems bad but not as bad as usual, as if its wickedness gets bounded by the mundaneness of the workplace.

The affective meanings produced by an action apply in the context of that action in that place at that time. Discerning a new action involving the same individuals transforms affective meanings again, as you rework the affective meanings produced by the last event. Consequently affective meanings produced by actions are short lived—transient.

Both pre-action feelings and the feelings emerging from the action have Evaluation, Potency, and Activity (EPA) components. A number of different mental processes transform the EPA values of pre-action feelings into EPA values of post-action feelings. The following sections discuss the most important processes discovered in impression-formation studies.

6.2.2 Stability

Impression formation always involves some stability. That is, your mind transfers some pre-action feeling toward an action element to the post-action feeling involving the same action element. For example, regardless of their behavior, you have a tendency to see actors as good after actions if the actors were good to begin with, and you tend to see actors as bad after actions if they were bad before the action.

In general, the goodness, powerfulness, and liveliness of actors, object persons, settings, and behaviors are stable to some degree.

6.2.3 Behavior Effects

A *morality effect* is one of the most important factors in impression formation. Evaluation of an actor's behavior influences how good or bad the actor seems after an action. For example, anyone helping another gets evaluative credit for engaging in a noble act. Anyone killing another is discredited for engaging in a horrific act.

Some of the potency of a behavior transfers to the actor, too. Actors seem more powerful when they engage in powerful behaviors.

Lively acts transfer activity back to the actor, and additionally make the actor seem more powerful; conversely quiet acts make the actor seem more inactive and powerless.

6.2.4 Object Diminishment

An individual loses potency merely by being the object of another's behavior. For example, consider John kissed Mary, and Mary kissed John, which could be two ways of looking at the same event. Both Mary and John might well think of self as actor while kissing, because being the object of the other's behavior makes one feel relatively weak and vulnerable.

Reduction of object potency is exacerbated when the actor's behavior is potent, because behavior potency impacts on the object person opposite to the way it impacts on the actor—strong acts make the object seem weaker. This is especially true when there is inconsistency between the potency of the actor and the act—an impotent actor behaving potently toward an object person makes the object person seem especially vulnerable. Think how inadequate a father would feel if his ten-year-old had to instruct him on the proper way to greet her teacher.

6.2.5 Consistencies

Consistency effects relate feelings regarding the evaluation, potency, or activity of two different action elements.

Behavior-object evaluation consistency. An actor who performs a bad act on a good object person violates a consistency principle—that good objects require good treatment, and that bad objects require bad treatment—so the actor seems bad not only because of the morality effect but additionally because of behavior-object inconsistency on the evaluation dimension.

Behavior-object evaluation consistency affects the goodness-badness of the actor, object, and behavior in an action. That is, if the goodness-badness of the behavior matches the goodness-badness of the object person, then actor, object, and behavior all seem nicer. If the behavior is inconsistent with the goodness-badness of the object, then actor, object, and behavior all seem less good.

Thus, for example, politicians like to be seen hugging and kissing babies because hugging and kissing is good, yielding a morality effect, but also because babies are nice so hugging and kissing babies earns extra credit by performing an act that is evaluatively consistent with the object. On the other hand, a picture of a politician shaking hands with a gangster is a political faux pas for the politician because it shows a good act being done to a bad object.

Actor-behavior evaluative consistency. Another consistency principle is that actors should behave in accordance with the way they are evaluated; not doing so gets them discredited. For example, for a politician's admirers, his kissing a baby ordinarily enhances evaluations of the politician not only because of the morality effect and the behavior-object evaluative consistency, but because the act is consistent with their feelings about the actor. However, it works differently if you hate the politician. Then, his kissing babies seems totally out of character—even sinister—so the inconsistency cancels the positive impact of the behavior.

Impressions of a behavior also are influenced by this effect. A good behavior seems defiled when used by an evil actor, and a bad behavior seems more honorable when performed by a valued actor.

Actor-behavior potency consistency. Consistency between the potency of the actor and the potency of the behavior increases the apparent powerfulness of the object person, and decreases the apparent powerfulness of the actor. This principle is relevant mainly for a very powerful actor who wants to maintain an aura of power: such a person should not engage in extremely strong acts because such acts make the actor seem desperate, and the object person seem invincible. Instead, very strong actors must act in moderately potent ways that confirm their potency without bordering on desperation. (No distinctly weak interpersonal behaviors are available in most cultures to enter into this process.)

6.2.6 Congruencies

Congruency principles relate feelings on two different EPA dimensions regarding two different action elements. Two such effects are especially important in impression formation.

Behavior evaluation and object potency congruency. This combination affects evaluations of actors in the following ways.

Mercifulness. Behaving nicely to weak objects makes an actor seem good. (Still another reason that politicians kiss babies!)

Courageousness. Directing bad acts to strong objects makes an actor seem brave. (So politicians love to attack big government!)

Sycophancy. Directing nice acts to strong objects makes an actor seem bad, like a toady.

Ruthlessness. Directing abusive acts toward weak objects makes an actor seem evil.

Behavior potency and object evaluation congruency. Combinations of behavior potency with object evaluation also affect evaluations of actors. However, there are just two conditions since behavior potency ranges from powerful to not-powerful, never all the way to powerless.

Righteousness. Performing potent actions on evil people can make an actor seem upright.

Impertinence. Performing potent actions on cherished people can make an actor seem improperly bold.

6.2.7 Balance

Balance effects relate feelings on an EPA dimension regarding all three core action elements—actor, behavior, and object. The set of feelings is balanced if all three are positive, or if any two are negative. For example, actors seem extra good if an action combines a positive actor, a positive behavior, and a positive object person.

Evaluation balance. In effect, this balance effect enhances, or lessens, evaluation consistency effects. That is, this balance effect increases the actor-behavior consistency effect when the object is a good person, and diminishes it when the object is a bad person. Similarly, the importance of the behavior-object consistency effect increases when the actor is a good person, but declines when the actor is bad.

Potency balance. This balance effect works inversely on actor evaluations. Powerful individuals seem less good when they direct powerful behaviors at each other; and powerless individuals also seem less good when they direct powerful behaviors at each other. Powerful individuals seem nicer if they direct potent acts at weak others or if weak individuals direct potent actions at them. Similarly weak individuals seem nicer if they direct powerful acts at powerful others, or have powerful others acting potently toward them. Assume, for example, that a toddler is weak, a father is powerful, and kissing is a deep, potent act. Then, a toddler kissing her father makes both child and parent seem very sweet.

6.2.8 States of Being

Impression formation results from actions, as just discussed. Impressions also form from observations about an actor's state of being—e.g., the father is angry—and from assertions that imply an actor's state of being—e.g., the angry father disciplined the child. States of being are identified by particularizing modifiers that refer to traits, biological characteristics, moral conditions, and moods.

Descriptions of states of being combine with an actor's identity to produce predictable outcomes, on all three EPA dimensions. The state of being generally has more impact on the outcome impression than the identity does. A consistency effect also operates on the evaluation dimension, such that good modifiers with good identities seem especially good.

6.2.9 Cross-Cultural Variations

Impression formation from social actions has been investigated in U.S., Canadian, and Japanese cultures. The major effects discussed above prevail in all three cultures, but some other relatively minor effects vary from one culture to another.

Impressions from assertions about states of being have been investigated in the U.S.A. and Japan, and a fair number of cultural variations have been found. For example, in Japanese culture, evaluation consistency between a state of being and identity is not so important in creating evaluation impressions as it is in U.S. culture, but potency consistency operates inversely in a significant way. That is, in Japan a potent actor in a potent state of being seems less good than the individual's identity suggests. For example, a sumo grand champion is quite esteemed in Japan, but a proud sumo grand champion is esteemed only slightly.

6.3 Impressions Versus Sentiments—Deflection

Likely actions create post-event impressions that match sentiments. An action that deflects impressions away from sentiments seems unlikely. Of course, any action deflects impressions away from sentiments to some degree, but the deflection is small in the case of likely actions and large in the case of unlikely actions.

For example, if you see a mother hugging her baby, the action creates impressions of mother and baby that probably are very close to your sentiments about mothers and babies. So this action seems likely, even to the point of being something you expect of mothers. On the other hand, seeing a physician ridicule a patient creates feelings that probably depart from your sentiments about physicians and patients, so this action seems unusual and unexpected. Occasionally an action wrenches your feelings very far from your sentiments, as in discovering that a mother murdered her baby; such an action makes the mother totally evil rather than nurturing, and this seems so unlikely that you have trouble believing such an action really happened. Similarly, experiencing a loved one dying creates an impression of the loved one very far from one's sentiment, and the event seems so impossible that the loved one may be conceived as still living, supernaturally.

Think of the distance between impression and sentiment as a quantity. If you add up the quantities for all of the elements in an event—actor, behavior, object, setting—you get a total called deflection. In general, the greater the deflection generated by an event, the less likely the event seems.

6.4 Identifying Behaviors

Mastering a language and learning its verbs gives you abundant cognitive frames to categorize sequences of perceived activity in culturally-standard ways. You do this very quickly, even though your language provides many hundreds of verbs.

Yet you often cannot make a final categorization on cognitive bases alone. Recalling the man-departing-from-woman example, the observed sequence of activity could fit a number of different interpretations: depart from, abandon, leave, desert, escape from, flee. You resolve the ambiguity affectively.

The behavior you finally choose to interpret a social action leads to impressions of the participants, to feelings about them. Within the constraints imposed by cognition, you choose the behavior that creates feelings that match your sentiments about the participants.

Thus, you may decide that the man abandoned the woman because that man is an enemy of yours. Or you may decide that the man fled the woman because earlier in the evening you identified that particular woman as an obnoxious drunk.

A complication that can arise is figuring out whether perceived activity is authentic—e.g., was the man just feigning leaving the woman? Most of the time you assume that settings are what they seem to be, people are who they say they are, and others' behaviors come from their hearts. However, the hypothesis of deception has to be considered now and then.

Another complication arises when you're in a group of people socially constructing an interpretation of an action. Different observers may forward different framings of what was perceived and debate with each other in order to arrive at a shared conception of what happened. For example, in the man-woman sequence, one observer may argue that the man and woman were not associated to begin with, in which case the interpretation of the man departing from the woman wouldn't be correct. Most of the time you assume that others have the same experiences as you, but now and then a check of that assumption reveals that it is not true, whereupon you and the others may work to achieve a consensual experience.

Social negotiations about the interpretation of actions are not strictly about cognitive matters. Emergent affective meanings change with different interpretations, so individuals also promote their own interpretation in order to confirm the sentiments invoked by their personal definitions of the situation.

6.5 Further Readings

Charles Fillmore presented a simple version of case grammar that still suffices for many social psychological analyses in his 1968 essay "The case for case." Fillmore and his colleagues now espouse frames, as surveyed in "FrameNet and Frame Semantics" (Fontenelle 2003).

The basic source on impression formation processes in English is the book, *Analyzing Social Interaction* (Smith-Lovin and Heise, 1988). Herman Smith and his colleagues have presented Japanese results in a series of articles (Smith 2002; Smith and Francis 2005; Smith, Matsuno and Ike 2001; Smith, Matsuno and Umino 1994).

7

Building Actions

Interpreting others' actions in familiar ways helps you experience life in terms of known categories and established sentiments. A still better way to have experiences affirming your knowledge and sentiments is to build events yourself. When you yourself are acting, you know what's happening, and your actions produce impressions that confirm your sentiments optimally.

Building an action requires filling the slots of a social action. Some key choices already are set by your definition of the situation—you know what setting you are in and what identities you and the other have. Your impetus to act implies that you are the actor and someone else is the object—the other person if you are interacting with one other individual. The remaining question is: What behavior should you perform?

7.1 Selecting a Behavior

Of all the behaviors you know—roughly speaking, all the verbs in your language—you immediately eliminate some because of your definition of the situation. A particular institution is implied by your recognition of the setting and the identities of those present. The acts associated with that institution are permissible, and unique acts of other institutions are not.

For example, if you are in an educational setting—say you're a professor with a student—then it is appropriate to perform the unique acts of the educational institution such as grading the student, or to perform acts that are appropriate in many institutions like advising, questioning, complimenting, admonishing, instructing, debating with, punishing, or sympathizing with the student. However, it is not appropriate to perform unique acts of other institutions, such as arresting, selling to, medicating, blessing, spanking, or making love to the student. A behavior that violates institutional boundaries constitutes a serious breach of ethics, if the behavior is not simply preposterous.

While your institutional context narrows the options, a great many acts still are left to choose from. How do you home in on the act that is right at the moment?

Affect does the work. Behaviors that best confirm your sentiments become psychologically available, and you select from this relatively small set the behavior that is most sensible in the circumstances.

Suppose, for example, that a father is on the brink of acting toward his son, and nothing has happened recently to create peculiar impressions of the two. Many behaviors are unthinkable because they would create impressions so remote from sentiments that the behaviors are emotionally and morally inconceivable. For instance, knife, make fun of, brutalize, molest, torture, choke, ridicule, whip, or scream at—none of these options even occurs to the father (assuming the father's sentiments are typically American) because such a behavior would deflect impressions of father and son far from sentiments.

Numerous less extreme behaviors also are out of mind for the father. A few instances are baby, tease, plead with, deride, silence, confine, argue with, criticize, or glower at. In normal circumstances, such options do not occur to the father because they transform impressions of self and other that are close to sentiments into impressions that deviate from sentiments. Engaging in such behaviors would create an action that feels anomalous and improbable.

Behaviors that are psychologically available to the father create impressions of father and son that are close to sentiments. Such behaviors include assist, explain something to, encourage, reason with, share something with, grin at, dine with, listen to, hug, compromise with, play with, or protect. These kinds of behaviors surface in the father's mind to spark initiation of his action.

Affective processing narrows the behavior options, perhaps to a dozen or so. What then determines the final selection? First, circumstances might instigate a logical sequence that selects one of the sentiment-confirming acts over others. For example, if the father perceives a threat to the son, then all other behavior options fade as the father moves directly into protecting his son. Second, a suggestion from someone else can elevate the imminence of an act. For example, watching a pre-school son trying to ride his first bike, a father might be tempted to encourage him, but mother's request—"Oh John, help him!"—elicits an act of assistance instead. Third, some sentiment-affirming actions might be eliminated from consideration because they are not feasible in the circumstances. The father cannot dine with his son if it no food is available, he cannot compromise with him if no request has been made, he cannot hug him if they are across the room from one another. Narrowed to just the feasible behaviors, the father might make his final selection arbitrarily—any institutionally-appropriate, feasible, and sentiment-affirming behavior is appropriate.

7.2 Social Interaction

When engaged in social interaction, you create actions that confirm the affective meanings of your own and others' identities. Other interactants in the situation operate the same way as you do, choosing actions that validate their sentiments about the identities they discern in the situation. Sequences of social interaction emerge as you and other individuals act on each other, transforming impressions of yourselves, all trying to consummate their sentiments in their experiences.

Consider a simple example. You are with your sweetheart, and each of you sees self and other as a sweetheart. With these identities, you and the other can perform many validating behaviors with each other, such as court, laugh with, speak to, desire sexually, embrace, compliment, satisfy, kiss, fondle, amuse, welcome, play with, caress, defend, please, sleep with, interest, treat, warn, or cheer.

Suppose you compliment your sweetheart. The action provides you with a feeling of satisfaction, and it makes your sweetheart feel charmed or gleeful. In response, suppose your sweetheart kisses you, an act giving your sweetheart satisfaction, while leaving you feeling pleased, perhaps merry. Exchanging such acts back and forth validates the meaning of sweetheart for each of you, in that the impressions created of each person match the sentiment associated with the sweetheart identity. The acts additionally produce emotions associated with the sweetheart relationship.

Interactions are not always so straightforward. For example, negative acts within a relationship damage both individuals so neither can serve as a resource for the other to regain goodness. Instead the interactants have to repair their damaged selves through a series of actions that edge them back toward normality.

Suppose your sweetheart meets you for a date wearing a new pair of shoes. The shoes strike you as so outlandishly silly looking that you break out laughing as you stare at them. However, a glance upward reveals that your sweetheart's face has tightened into resentment, and you hear the words, "Done ridiculing me?" Your jaw drops as you realize that is exactly what you just did. Feeling awful, you sheepishly accept your sweetheart's lecture about fashion, or about attending to others' feelings, or the solemn forgiveness your sweetheart offers to you. Still feeling melancholy you offer your heartfelt assurance of love. After some poignant hugging, then some exultant kisses, the two of you finally get back to your normal sweetheart relationship! The initial negative act continues to affect impressions, behaviors, and emotions for several rounds of interaction.

Negative actions within a positive relationship generally occur because different interactants frame an action differently. That is the case above where one sweetheart laughs until the other sweetheart lets it be known that a laugh-at is what is happening, rather than laugh-with! Since others must interpret your actions, they may find a different meaning than you intended.

Another kind of complication in interaction arises when just one individual's identity has been invalidated, and the individual uses a relationship as a resource to repair the discombobulated self. Consider this example, which has been demonstrated in an experiment. Suppose you are a student taking a test, and the secretary administering the test interrupts you and demeans you for using a pen rather than a pencil to mark your answer sheet. When the secretary is gone, you grin at your friend taking the test with you, maybe even compliment some article of your friend's clothing. Your behavior is unusually positive after depreciation by the secretary, whereas before you were satisfied just to sit with your friend, and chit-chat a bit. On the other hand, imagine the same scene where the other student in the room with you is awaiting a disciplinary conference in which he is likely to be expelled from school and even charged criminally. Now after the secretary berates you, you may glance at the other, but overall you try to avoid interaction. In the first scene your friend is a resource for pulling your self-evaluation up, but in the second scene interacting with the deviant could only make impressions of yourself sink lower.

Additional complications in social interaction arise when one individual defines the situation differently than the others do, or when an individual defines the situation the same way as others do but has unshared sentiments about some of the salient identities. Examples of these kinds of predicament are given in later sections.

7.2.1 Groups

In a group of three or more individuals you can chose your partner for actions. Whenever feasible, you chose interaction partners so as to experience actions that maximally confirm your sentiments.

One surprising implication of this principle is that individuals with negative self-evaluation prefer to interact with others who criticize them, even though the derogations are emotionally painful! That is because being criticized is an experience that confirms a negative self-sentiment. On the other hand, individuals who have positive self-esteem prefer to be with others who appreciate them, since being appreciated is an experience that confirms a positive self-sentiment. Experiments have substantiated these outcomes among people with varying self-sentiments, who had to decide whether critics or appreciators would be their future interaction partners.

A similar principle explains how friendship cliques form in groups. Your identity in a group will be confirmed best by affiliating with people having compatible identities, and may be disconfirmed by affiliating with people with incompatible identities. Moreover, ideas also can be compatible or incompatible: your identity is confirmed by propounding ideas having an affective meaning that resonates with your identity, and your identity can be disconfirmed by touting ideas that do not fit it.

Accordingly, in a community of individuals whose identities have varying levels of evaluation and potency, we can expect a number of cliques to form, each with a preferred ideology. Individuals whose identities have high potency and positive evaluation will align together and support ideals like altruism, social progress, material success, or loyalty to authority. Another clique may form containing individuals with identities of medium potency and positive evaluation who support equalitarianism, emotional supportiveness, trust in others, or self-inquiry. Individuals with low potency identities may form a clique forwarding identification with the underprivileged, liberalism, rejection of authority and conformity, or rejection of material success. Another clique may form containing individuals with identities that are high potency and negatively evaluated, these individuals being devoted to tough-minded assertiveness, restraint, rugged individualism, isolationism, or self-sacrifice.

7.2.2 Avoiding Diminishment

Most people have high self-esteem and a sense of personal efficacy, which translates into their maintaining identities that are positively evaluated, with high potency. Maintaining potency of self creates a quandary when such people get together in interaction. Each wants to be the actor rather than the object in the next action, in order to avoid object-diminishment during impression formation. But how can everyone be an actor and no one be an object? The predicament has a number of different resolutions.

One possibility is an interaction peppered with interruptions. You start a behavior like teaching the other something, and suddenly the other is congratulating you on a recent success, then trying to lead you toward something the other favors. You interrupt the other's maneuver by renewing your act of educating the other. And so on—each trying to substitute an action to confirm one's own potency before being diminished as the object of the other's action. Such interactions are invigorating while each individual perceives the self as dominating the process, but the interaction becomes frustrating and stressful for a party who gets overpowered.

A compromise solution to the predicament is provided by the sophisticated system of turn-taking offered within contemporary culture. Some actions require taking turns as part of their structure, such as questioning, requesting, or inviting. Beyond that, completion of any action opens the floor—to use the language of formal meetings, and at that point individuals other than the current actor get a chance to enact the next event. Turn-taking does not keep one from being diminished as the object of others' actions, but it does offer the opportunity for quick redress by taking the role of actor after diminishment.

Sometimes individuals are able to perform one action collaboratively. For example, as two friends regale themselves with their memory of some joint experience, they may unfold the story by passing the speaker role back and forth, sentences begun by one may be finished by the other, and some sentences may be spoken in chorus. Since both are performing the same general action, each produces the same potent impression of self. Of course, such improvisations work only when both individuals know their topic equally well and could perform the whole sequence alone, allowing them to contribute equally.

Multi-person routines in organizational settings provide the benefits of collaborative actions. In this case, individuals all have distinct roles, which they know by virtue of training, and the action they perform together requires the contributions of all. For example, an injured child delivered to a hospital emergency room initiates a bustle of activity by nurses and doctors in which each makes their standard contribution to a standard medical routine. Each individual reasonably views the self as actor in this event, and thus each enjoys the sense of potency of performing the overall action—that is, each nurse and doctor personally gets the fulfillment of saving the child.

7.3 Social Roles

Consider Jim.
- In his identity of physician, Jim medicates other people.
- In his identity of weekend football player, Jim tackles others.
- In his identity of lover, Jim kisses another individual.

You have to know Jim's identity in a given situation in order to know what behavior Jim might do next. You can predict behavior better if you also know the identities of

Jim's interaction partners and if you are aware of recent happenings. For example, Jim in his role of physician is more likely to medicate patients than to medicate nurses, and Jim is especially likely to medicate a patient after listening to the patient's complaints.

Each identity defines a different social role—a different set of likely behaviors. Roles are the functioning part of social institutions like medicine, law, family, religion, education, or commerce.

Roles within institutions often involve technical performances that require trained judgment and rationality, so you might think that affect has little relevance in understanding the behaviors of people acting in institutional roles. However, expressive actions grounded in affect are ubiquitous, and a great deal of institutional functioning is affect instigated.

Identities and behaviors in social institutions like medicine, law, and business have been shaped by institutional participants so that the actions required of institutional roles are actions that confirm affective meanings. Thus as participants act spontaneously on an affective basis, they produce actions that rationally contribute to instrumental goals. Following are some examples of how this works.

7.3.1 Medicine

Imagine that you are a doctor interacting with another doctor. You want to behave in a way that produces impressions of both parties that match the sentiment for doctor—quite good and potent and somewhat active. A congenial behavior is required to produce a good impression of both. Your behavior must be potent to affirm your own potency, but not so potent that it diminishes the potency of the other doctor. The activity of your act should approximately match the fundamental activity of doctors in order to produce a somewhat active impression of both individuals.

So what kinds of acts fit this profile, acknowledging that you do not want to perform a specialized behavior of some institution other than medicine? Some prime possibilities are answer, confer with, consult with, discuss something with, remind, show something to, or speak to. Any of these behaviors produces impressions of both parties that are quite close to the sentiment for a doctor.

Which behavior would you actually perform? Logic and rationality come into play at this point. You cannot answer the other if the other asked no question, you cannot remind the other if nothing is imminent, and you cannot show something if there is nothing notable to see. On the other hand, when the pre-condition for any one of these behaviors is fulfilled, then the behavior becomes highly motivated in a doctor-doctor interaction. For example, during an operation, you certainly will remind the other doctor to remove an overlooked sponge before suturing.

General behaviors like speaking-to have no specific pre-conditions, but they do require reasoning to implement. That is, your interaction partner will presume that anything you say makes sense if examined carefully enough, so you are obligated to speak in ways that do make sense. For example, as a doctor you cannot say "Sycamore trees" to another doctor if that relates to nothing in the situation or in your shared pasts. Your sanity would come into question if you did such things!

Other behaviors in a doctor-doctor interaction are eliminated by principles regarding the behavior's application. For example, injecting with medicine is an act in a doctor's toolkit that generally creates the proper impression of a doctor. However, doctors may inject patients only, so the act cannot be done to another doctor, unless the other loses the doctor identity and becomes a patient.

Continuing to imagine yourself as a doctor, consider your interaction with a nurse. Many behavior options are the same as with a doctor, but other behaviors that were in the background of a doctor-doctor interaction become salient in a doctor-nurse interaction, because sentiments about nurses are different from the doctor sentiment. For example, instructing the nurse comes to fore as an act that confirms both identities well and may meet functional demands. Friendly acts of flattery, comforting, or sympathizing also seem more appropriate in the doctor-nurse relationship.

The patient identity is less valued and less potent than the identities of doctor or nurse. Consequently as a doctor you can maintain the patient identity with acts that are less amiable and more potent than those used toward doctors and nurses, and this difference again changes the salience of behaviors within your doctor's toolkit. You may caution and warn a patient, or advise, appeal to, counsel, give instructions to, or suggest something to the patient. The options of medicating the patient or injecting the patient with medicine are prominent and sensible, as is putting the individual to bed. Of course, as doctor you continually must maintain the positivity of your doctor identity, so relatively authoritarian acts need to be interspersed with empathic acts of accommodating and excusing, agreeing with, apologizing to, chatting with, or soothing the patient.

Many behaviors toward a patient are completely out of mind for you as doctor, because they create impressions totally contrary to sentiments about doctors and patients. Acts of purposeful injury, hurt, and harm are so affectively inappropriate that their performance would seem immoral or insane, and, indeed, the Hippocratic Oath for physicians includes the vow never to do harm to anyone. Close behind in affectively inappropriate acts are belittling, cursing, degrading, insulting, ridiculing, screaming at, threatening, or tormenting. Such behaviors toward a patient are out mind for a doctor because they create such a bad impression of the actor, at odds with the sentiment that doctors are fundamentally good.

The patient as much as the doctor wants impressions to match sentiments, and for the most part that means taking a passive role in the relationship, letting the doctor maintain the high evaluation and potency of the doctor identity. If the patient does act, it must be with low potency behaviors that create impressions unthreatening to the doctor's authority—acts like obeying, minding, watching, or requesting something from.

7.3.2 Law

Consider sentiments about some key characters in a courtroom. A judge is good, very powerful, and a bit quiet. A lawyer is good, somewhat less potent than a judge, and active. A prosecuting attorney is not nice but not awful either, with potency between a judge's and lawyer's, and activity comparable to a lawyer's. A defendant is slightly negative in evaluation, powerless, and a bit quiet. In relationship to a lawyer, though, a defendant has the identity of client, which is good, somewhat potent, and somewhat active.

Now consider how the sentiments for the identities order available acts in the legal toolkit of behaviors so as to constitute the role of each officer of the court when acting toward the defendant.

The judge has to create self-impressions of goodness, a high level of potency, and reserve, while maintaining the defendant's affectively-neutral sentiment. Passive observation of the defendant accomplishes this: observing, inspecting, glancing at, or looking at. Other possibilities include supervisory actions of quieting, addressing, briefing, or correcting the defendant. In appropriate circumstances, the judge might also excuse, comfort, apologize to, or exonerate the defendant.

The lawyer has to create impressions of self and client that are good, potent, and lively. Acts that do this include cuing, prompting, directing, or urging the client. Privately the lawyer can produce the right impressions by interviewing, questioning, challenging, or cautioning the client. For public display, the lawyer's sentiment-confirming acts include lauding, excusing, or exonerating the client.

To confirm sentiments about self and the defendant, the prosecuting attorney must create impressions that are non-positive in evaluation, with the prosecutor seeming powerful and lively while the defendant seems weak and passive. Acts of prosecuting and convicting the defendant accomplish this, as well as specific acts like commanding, confronting, cross-examining, disagreeing with, interrogating, rebuking, reproaching, or smirking at.

Recent events can change saliencies of acts. For example, suppose that an overwrought defendant defies a judge's direct order to remain seated. The defendant's action creates an impression of the judge as less good than a judge should be, and considerably less potent. The action also makes the defendant seem worse than a defendant should be, and insufficiently powerless and quiet. What can the judge to do to turn these anomalous impressions into impressions that better match sentiments about judges and defendants?

Because both judge and defendant have declined in goodness, the judge has to act less pleasantly than usual—any meliorative effects of acting nicely would be neutralized by the inconsistency of acting nicely toward this fractious defendant. Because the judge is below par in potency and the defendant seems too powerful, the judge must act forcefully in order to restore customary power relations. Additionally, the judge must avoid any freneticism in order to maintain the standard reserve of a judge.

These demands change the saliencies of acts for the judge with regard to the defendant. Now staring down, dissuading, or fining the defendant are prominent possibilities for the judge—acts that ordinarily are not salient. In response to the defendant's defiance, the judge also has more impetus to convict the defendant.

Thus, though the same acts generally are available to all officers of the court, the need of each party to maintain different sentiments about self and the defendant and to transform impressions created by recent events makes different sub-sets of acts salient for each participant, thereby defining the unique role of each court officer.

7.3.3 Work Roles

Suppose you are an employer and you see Jones as an employee, and Jones's definitions are parallel to yours. Sentiments associated with employer and employee are similar on evaluation and activity: both are good and somewhat active. However, the two identities differ in potency, with employer being quite powerful and employee being neither powerless nor powerful.

When acting toward Jones, you have to maintain the goodness and liveliness of both parties while producing impressions of yourself as very powerful and of Jones as non-powerful. Salient acts for you include supervisory acts like supervise, assist, guide, remind, direct, inform, explain something to, give instructions to, show something to, caution, or warn; fellowship acts like chat with, talk to, reassure, encourage, urge on, advise, accommodate, agree with, or flatter; and administrative acts like interview, employ, compensate, promise something to, confront, reason with, or negotiate with. These are the kinds of acts by which you produce impressions matching sentiments in this relationship.

When Jones acts toward you, the demands are the same—make both parties seem good and lively, while making you substantially more powerful than Jones. However, Jones acting puts you—the more powerful individual—in the object position, subject to object diminishment, so Jones has to forego acts that are too potent. Behaviors that produce the proper impressions include instrumental acts like serve, talk shop with, listen to, answer, ask about something, consult with, show something to, remind, or caution; and relational acts like chat with, jest with, console, agree with, exalt, confess to, apologize to, reassure; make up with, or compromise with.

Thus, when you both try to confirm sentiments about employer and employee, you and Jones perform normal workplace roles.

Now suppose you still see yourself as an employer, but you see Jones as a loafer. Jones, on the other hand, sees himself as an employee, but he sees you as a scrooge because you've put a lid on his salary in order to cut costs. These conflicting definitions of the situation introduce complications into interactions between the two of you.

You still have to produce impressions of yourself as good, very potent, and lively, but simultaneously your behavior has to create impressions of Jones that confirm him as a loafer—bad, weak, and very inactive. Acts that now become salient as best achieving this include observing, quieting, questioning, or dressing down Jones.

Suppose you make a point of observing Jones, and Jones—aware of your observation—responds. Jones feels inadequately appreciated by your action, yet at the same time Jones' impression of you does not seem nearly negative enough to him, since a scrooge is quite bad, impotent, and a bit inactive. Jones has to choose an act that will transform his current impressions into new impressions that are closer to the sentiments associated with employee and scrooge. Salient acts to accomplish this include prompting you about something, questioning you, sounding you out, or toadying up to you.

Say Jones prompts you. Having a loafer prompt you produces an impression of you that is insufficiently good and potent, and it makes Jones seem insufficiently bad, weak, and inactive. Now you have to do something to get back your dominance and status, while pushing Jones back into his loafer character. The options are few and none of them are entirely effective. Quieting Jones is about the best you can do.

At that point Jones perceives that a scrooge has quieted an employee. Accordingly Jones feels increasingly devalued and diminished, and he sees you as increasingly distant from the venality and spinelessness appropriate to a scrooge. Among the acts that Jones might use to repair his perceived state of affairs are reproaching, admonishing, or rebuking you.

Jones reproaching you pushes you over the edge! That action creates impressions of Jones that are completely out of character for a loafer—insufficiently bad, weak, and lazy. The action also creates an impression of you as an employer that is far too deficient in goodness, power, and activity. You must convert those impressions to new impressions that are more in line with sentiments towards employers and loafers. Among the behaviors that come to your mind are disciplining Jones, even firing him.

In just such a way can unshared definitions of situations wreak havoc in work worlds, as individuals try to confirm their conflicting sentiments.

7.3.4 Macroactions

Individuals occupying institutional roles of authority often accomplish interpersonal actions through the participation of other people. For example, a professor grading student papers in a large class may examine no essays at all, but instead instigate reading and grading of essays by multiple teaching assistants. A business executive contracting with an official in another firm may talk on the telephone and provide a signature, but leave detailed paper work to aides and secretaries.

Macroactions are acts that are initiated by an actor but performed by someone else or by a social organization.

One difference between macroactions and individual behaviors is that macroactions may be more intricate than individual actions, because an organization can focus specialists within a division of labor on the behavioral goal. Another difference is that macroactions may span a longer period of time than individual actions, as individuals and sub-groups within the organization coordinate their work into a cumulative sequence that yields a final product. Thus interactions conducted via macroactions proceed slower and perhaps with more far reaching consequences than ordinary face-to-face interaction.

Yet the affective basis of interaction is the same with macroactions as with individual behaviors. Macroactions have sentiments attached to them; macroactions deployed in events generate impressions of actors and objects; and actors use macroactions to maintain the affective meanings of themselves and their interaction partners.

International relations involves macroaction exchanges. Representatives of a nation—presidents, prime ministers, ambassadors, etc.—take on their nation's identity in interchanges with representatives of other nations and select behaviors to affirm the sentiments attached to nation identities, or to repair impressions from events threatening those sentiments. Nations with positive mutual sentiments engage in sustained cooperation, and nations that have negative sentiments in their relation with each other engage in persistent conflict.

Actions that are inconsistent with nation identities cause disconfirmation of sentiments, and such actions instigate new actions to repair the problem. Negative events between cooperative nations are redeemed quickly by some exceptionally positive action. Positive events between hostile nations quickly get nullified by some new outrage.

Such processes change mainly at turning points provided by elections, coups or other forms or regime change. However, the other party in the relationship has to accept that the relationship has changed, or else a turning point only leads to unshared definitions of the relationship, with each party struggling to affirm its own definition.

7.3.5 Informal Roles

Many of the interactions you have in everyday life do not involve institutional roles. You find yourself in generic identities that fit any situation—like man or woman, pal, or advisor—and you deal with others who also have such identities. You may not think of yourself as taking on negative identities, but you encounter other people who behave like a prude or a jerk or a party-pooper or a bully, etc., so informal negative identities are operative in your everyday life, too.

The goal of matching impressions to sentiments generates behaviors associated with informal roles as well as behaviors attached to institutional roles. For example, knowing that individuals try to confirm the sentiments of their identities, you expect buddies to be supportive of one another, bullies to be aggressive, novices to kid around, and jerks—well, you expect jerks will act like jerks. Advisors act sympathetic, loners show independence; and behaviors of party-poopers and fuddy-duddies exasperate those who are with them. Moreover, behavior constructed to confirm sentiments adjusts in plausible ways, depending on one's interaction partner: e.g., a man shows excitement and helpfulness with valued others; he is brusque and uncompromising with those he scorns. Predicted responses to deviance in informal relationships make sense, too. For example, an individual who gets caught lying to her roommate may cause the other to reproach her.

In general, as individuals act spontaneously on an affective basis in informal relationships, they produce actions that express and implement those relationships.

7.4 Deviance

What is deviant action? One answer is that deviance involves a behavior that is negatively evaluated.

Negatively evaluated behaviors include some despicable acts—e.g., lying to, stealing from, torturing, and murdering—but negative evaluation of behavior alone does not guarantee social deviance. Babbling to or glaring at someone are negatively evaluated, but they are not villainous. Moreover, some negatively evaluated behaviors are legitimate actions for normal actors in certain institutions. Judges are supposed to convict, fine, and sentence; professors should flunk some people; police can properly arrest, confine, and interrogate suspects; those in charge of discipline are expected to punish and silence others. When these negatively-evaluated behaviors are directed at deviants, the actions are not deviant.

Deviance also has been interpreted as rare action, an idea that relates neatly to the issue of deflection. Deflection predicts the subjective likelihood of an event, and events that seem unlikely usually are fairly rare.

Most large-deflection actions combine a negatively evaluated behavior with positively valued actors or objects—e.g., the salesclerk cheated the child; the athlete raped the coed; the uncle beat his niece—and all such actions do seem very unlikely and deviant. So far, so good.

The trouble with this approach to defining deviance is that good actions performed by deviants—for example, a mugger helping a child—also deflect meanings and therefore must be deviant because they are unlikely actions. However, it doesn't really make sense to call good actions deviant, even if bad individuals perform them. Moreover, some positive behaviors, like God forgives the sinner, also produce moderate deflection. Individuals involved in such events may find such experiences extraordinary, but they do not ordinarily think of themselves as being involved in deviance.

Another problem is that villainous behavior among deviants does not generate much deflection: such actions seem likely. For example, a pimp punching a prostitute produces little deflection: that kind of behavior is expected from a pimp, and such a predicament is to be expected for a prostitute. Nevertheless the action would be deviant by most people's standards.

In 1964 U.S. Supreme Court Justice Potter Stewart despaired at defining pornography objectively, but famously said "I know it when I see it." Similarly, deviant actions cannot be defined objectively, but people know them when they see them. Constructionists flip this notion imaginatively, arguing that deviance comes into existence when people identify actions as deviant, especially people who have authority—like Supreme Court justices.

7.4.1 Interactions With Deviants

Foregoing the question of what constitutes deviant action, turn instead to the question of whether anything is special about interactions with deviants. For practical purposes, consider deviants to be individuals occupying negatively evaluated identities. This is not quite true, since some negatively evaluated identities are non-deviant (e.g., victim, slave). However, all deviants have negatively evaluated identities in the general culture.

Having a negative sentiment about an identity allows you to predict illicit actions and to sense risks intuitively. For example, knowing that muggers are bad, potent, and active, you expect them to bully, steal, rape, and kill, and you know you are in danger if a mugger is present.

When interacting with normal individuals, deviants validate their identities at the expense of the normal individuals, who are disconfirmed by the malevolent acts of the deviants.

For example, suppose a woman encounters a mugger. As soon as she realizes the other's identity, she expects unpleasant actions from him. At first she may not be intimidated, responding to his first approach by trying to dissuade him from harming her. Oddly this somewhat negative action of hers makes the mugger seem less villainous, and his response is to show his true vicious nature by threatening, pushing, attacking the woman. Sensing that the scene is getting out of hand, the woman now feels terrified. Yet despite her plummeting emotions, her behavioral inclinations continue to be valiant as she tries to maintain the strength and goodness of her identity as a woman. She still might try acts like persuading, exonerating, or converting the mugger. Such resolute behavior lets her feel more in control with emotions like indignation and scorn, even as she implicitly knows her action will trigger further aggressive behavior from the mugger.

On the other hand, the woman has the potential for re-casting herself as a victim. If she does so, her courage would be gone and her predicament in some ways worse! As a victim her behavior options are mainly begging and beseeching, while the mugger's options with a victim expand to a variety of violent and sexual acts. Curiously, even though the objective behavior expectations are worse in her role of victim, her emotions are mollified somewhat. Resigning herself to the role of victim replaces terror with anxiety, tenseness, and even anger.

Normal individuals cannot confirm themselves well in interactions with deviants. Even trying to do so emboldens the deviants to perform worse behaviors than usual.

7.4.2 Interactions Among Deviants

Cultural sentiments about deviants have evolved to make the characters predictable in their interactions with normal people. Normal people have no contact with the underworlds of deviance, and so they cannot adjust their sentiments in order to better predict the interactions of deviants among themselves. Nevertheless, our sentiments provide us with fantasies about what happens in deviant worlds. We easily imagine that deviants betray each other, frustrate each other, ridicule each other, exact vengeance on each other—plots like you see on television soap operas. Additionally we imagine that deviants often have positive emotions as they do these malevolent acts!

Our fantasies about deviants' interactions with each other are not always correct. Deviants sometimes get together in communities and normalize their sentiments about their deviant activities. The result is an unorthodox world from the standpoint of outsiders—a world where deviant people and actions are valued positively—as discussed in the chapter on sub-cultures.

However, some deviants do follow scripts provided by the general culture as they interact with one another. The key requirement is that the individuals are trying to maintain negative sentiments about themselves. More on this will follow in the chapter on selves.

7.5 Further Readings

The idea that actions are created to produce familiar experiences comes from William Powers, *Behavior: The Control of Perception* (1973). The impact of Powers' cybernetic model on sociology is surveyed in *Purpose, Meaning, and Action: Control Systems Theories in Sociology*, edited by Kent McClelland and Thomas Fararo (2006).

William Carter, Dawn Robinson, and Lynn Smith-Lovin (2006) showed that individuals act to protect both their own and others' identities, in their article "Restoring the challenged identity of others: Predicting restorative behaviors."

The experiment relating to responses during a test was conducted by Beverly Wiggins and is reported in *Analyzing Social Interactions* (Smith-Lovin and Heise,1988). An experiment showing that individuals prefer to interact with others who confirm their identities, even if the experiences are emotionally painful, was conducted by Dawn Robinson and Lynn Smith-Lovin, and reported in their 1992 article, "Selective interaction as a strategy for identity maintenance: An affect control model."

Dawn Robinson argued that cliques emerge from identity confirmation in her 1996 article, "Identity and friendship: Affective dynamics and network formation." Robert Freed Bales related self-sentiment types with ideological positions in various books, such as *Social Interaction Systems: Theory and Measurement* (1999).

Smith-Lovin and Robinson (1992) provided a detailed discussion of conversational tactics in their book chapter, "Gender and conversational dynamics."

Workplace conflicts caused by disparate sentiments have been discussed by Andreas Schneider (2002a) in his article, "Computer simulation of behavior prescriptions in multi-cultural corporations," and by Herman Smith in "Predicting stress in American-Japanese business relations" (Smith 1995).

The concept of macroaction was developed by Alex Durig and myself (Heise and Durig 1997) in "A frame for organizational actions and macroactions." Affective control of inter-nation macroactions was analyzed by Steven Lerner and myself (Heise and Lerner 2006) in "Affect control in international interactions." I reported additional analyses of international relations in "Sentiment formation in social interaction" (Heise 2006).

8

Emotions

Far from being primitive reflexes that interfere with social process (a view that once was common), emotions are vital for social organization. Emotions allow individuals to sense structure and change in social relationships.

8.1 Emotions as Signals

An emotion translates the impression of you created by an event into a physical feeling that lets you sense the event's impact viscerally. Additionally, your facial expression and other somatic manifestations of your emotion are visible to others, allowing them to form an impression of you that reflects your internal assessment of the scene.

For example, if an event makes you feel especially pleasant, strong, and lively, you acquire the glow and smiley face of happiness. Your emotion display lets others identify you as happy, yielding an impression of you as being especially pleasant, strong, and lively in the circumstances.

Thus, your emotions help others figure out how you define situations and how you assess recent events. (Sometimes you yourself consider your emotions to better understand your interpretations of situations and events!) Similarly, others' emotions help you figure out how they interpret a situation and recent happenings.

Can you use emotions to communicate a particular impression to others—like being especially pleasant, strong, and lively, even if you don't really feel happy? Yes. People sometimes construct emotion displays like they are supposed to have in a situation, and sometimes they show a false emotion to mislead others about their private assessments of a situation. Moreover, some businesses require employees to display emotions that they may not feel, in order to make customers feel good about themselves—businesses that provide "service with a smile"!

However, displaying inauthentic emotion is work—masking the emotion you really feel, and then shaping your face and body and voice to simulate a different emotion. Your real emotion can slip out despite your efforts to suppress it, and your simulated emotion can fall apart without guidance from a real internal state. In fact, an effective way to display an inauthentic emotion is actually to experience the desired emotion by reliving some scene where you had that emotion. This technique is taught to aspiring thespians in the method school of acting.

Table 8-1. Sample emotions organized in terms of evaluation, potency, and activity

Profile	Emotions, From Quiescent to Activated
Pleasant*	peaceful, serene, humble, touched, thankful, contented, pleased, glad, proud, delighted, happy, thrilled, ecstatic
Unpleasant, Superior	sorry, upset, disgusted, spiteful, indignant, contemptuous, aggravated, mad, alarmed, irate, furious, enraged
Unpleasant, Vulnerable	depressed, blue, disheartened, sickened, ashamed, embarrassed, worried, frightened, terrified, horrified, agitated, panicked

* English provides no names for pleasant emotions that involve vulnerability.

8.2 Impressions and Emotions

Different emotions have different levels of evaluation (pleasantness vs. unpleasantness), potency (superiority vs. vulnerability), and activity (activation vs. quiescence). Table 8-1 illustrates how emotions vary on these dimensions.

The different emotions create a variety of impressions when combined with an identity. Here are some examples.

- A happy doctor seems very pleasant, potent, and lively.
- An angry doctor seems somewhat unpleasant, neither strong nor weak, and neither lively nor quiet.
- A depressed doctor seems unpleasant, neither strong nor weak, and quiet.
- A happy invalid seems neither pleasant nor unpleasant, neither strong nor weak, and neither lively nor quiet.
- An angry invalid seems unpleasant, weak, and neither lively nor quiet.
- A depressed invalid seems unpleasant, very weak, and very quiet.

The pleasantness, superiority, and activation of your emotion at the moment reflect whether the current event is making you seem especially nice or awful, potent or impotent, and lively or quiet. If an event makes you seem especially good, potent, and active then you feel an emotion like happiness. If the event makes you seem unusually bad and lively and not too impotent, then you feel an emotion like anger. If the event makes you feel bad and lively and helpless then you feel an emotion like terror.

Your identity as well as your impression of self also is involved in your emotion. For example, you may look somewhat positive in a situation and yet feel an unpleasant emotion, if someone's action creates an impression of you that is not as good as your identity warrants.

Example: it's your birthday and your sweetheart gives you an unsigned mass-produced birthday card—that's all. Your sweetheart remembered your birthday, which creates a somewhat positive impression of you. But the impression created is so much less than you deserve as a sweetheart. No present? Not even a note or signature on the card? You're indignant! Or perhaps you now worry about the relationship.

Events involving you produce impressions of who you seem to be, and your identity defines who you are supposed to be. Your emotion connects the two. Your emotion, combined with your identity, creates the impression of you that is emerging in the current event. The impression generated by the conjunction of your emotion and identity duplicates the impression of you generated by the event.

Thus, seeing your emotion and knowing your identity, others can infer what kind of impression you think you are making in the scene. Or, combining your emotion with their own impression of how you are faring, others can infer what identity you're trying to maintain.

8.3 Characteristic and Structural Emotions

An event producing impressions that perfectly confirm an individual's identity would generate an emotion characteristic of the individual's identity. For example, a gangster getting perfect confirmation would feel alarm. A prostitute perfectly confirmed would feel agitation. A heroine getting perfect confirmation would feel joy. A perfectly confirmed minister would feel thankfulness.

Feelings get tugged away from characteristic emotions in actual interactions. You typically have to forego confirming your own identity perfectly in order to confirm the identities of your interaction partners simultaneously. Events created to confirm both identities as much as possible produce impressions that do not confirm either of the identities perfectly.

A structural emotion is the emotion you experience when you are in a specific identity, your partner is in a complementary identity, and your interaction together is confirming each individual's identity as much as possible. A structural emotion gives specific emotional flavor to the different kinds of relationships that you have while occupying an identity. For example, a minister with a sinner does not feel a minister's characteristic emotion of thankfulness, but instead feels indignation as interaction with the sinner unfolds. In his or her personal relationship with God, the minister enjoys emotions of satisfaction and reverence.

8.3.1 Solidarity

Individuals typically have different emotional experiences when they are in situations where everyone has a different identity. Divergence in emotions encourages the individuals to view themselves as autonomous.

However, suppose that everyone has the same identity, and all are interacting as a group with an external entity. Then everyone experiences the same structural emotion, and the consonance of emotion yields a sense of unified consciousness, a feeling of one-ness with the group. Add a conviction that the shared identity gives all a common motive with regard to the external entity, and a sense of solidarity emerges.

Crowds sometimes put everyone into a single identity, all relating to an outside entity, in a setting where individuals can personally observe the concert of parallel emotions and actions in others. Thus, crowd experiences can be transcendental, making you feel connected to others.

8.4 Emotions And Motivation

Humans act to maintain meanings, including their sentiments about themselves and others. This motivational axiom can be translated into emotion terms, as follows. You strive to experience the structural emotion for the relationship in which you find yourself, and you act to eliminate disparate emotions.

This view of emotions as motives implies that an emotion—other than a desired structural emotion—instigates behavior that is opposite in nature to the emotion producing it.

For example, consider feeling jealous. For most people a flash of jealousy signals that events have made one seem less good and more vulnerable than is warranted by one's identity in a relationship. To restore the usual valued and potent sense of self, one might engage in some affectionate behavior toward a loved one—for instance, hugging and caressing one's sweetheart. So jealousy is followed by predictable behavior, but the relation between the emotion and behavior is oppositional—agreeable behavior follows the disagreeable emotion.

Yet we sometimes think of emotions, as causing behaviors that are consistent with the emotions—jealous people acting vindictive, depressed people disengaging, elated people regaling their associates.

Emotions become straightforward motivational states when they get incorporated into identity. For example, an individual starts acting not just as a husband but as a jealous husband, or a depressed husband, or an elated husband. An emotion amalgamated with an identity indicates a mood—a temporary particularization of identity.

Individuals act to confirm their moods. Thus, mood-generated behavior fits with the mood in a straightforward way—vindictiveness confirming a jealous mood, disengagement confirming a depressed mood, regaling others confirming an elated mood. Of course, the manner of behaving during a mood varies with different partners and changing circumstances, just as behavior produced by an institutional identity varies in different conditions. But overall the mood generates behavior that befits the mood.

8.5 Stress

Deflection arises when impressions produced by an event differ from sentiments. Deflection that cannot be resolved produces psychological stress, a serious condition that can undermine one's health.

Usually deflection gets allayed after a few more events occur. However, deflection from some events persists over time.

For example, a loved one dying is high-deflection event because it creates an impression of the loved one far from one's sentiment about that individual. The deflection lasts because it is difficult to get another event that terminates the death event, or ameliorates it. Interaction with the loved one is impossible, and interactions with others do not change the aberrant impression of the loved one. Since it cannot be put into the past, the death gets relived over and over. Eventual relief awaits fading of the event in time, or imagining supernatural events that undo the aberrant impression of the loved one, or lowering one's sentiment about the loved one in order to have a sentiment closer to the impression left by death.

Another example: a professor is teaching a seminar and her students turn out to be resolute underachievers. The seminar starts okay, but aberrant impressions soon develop from classroom interactions, for both the professor and the students. Trying desperately to repair their identities, the professor acts increasingly authoritarian while the students alternately fawn and grouse. Nearly every action of professor and students makes deflection climb because disconfirmation is built into the relationship between a professor and underachievers. The end of the semester is a relief for all.

Deflection might continue unresolved, thereby turning into stress, because:

- The individual is chronically involved in situations where others define the situation differently. Flight attendants are an example: they see some passengers as rude oafs, but these passengers see themselves as privileged members of an elite class, and the passengers are supported by airline managers who require attendants to provide service with a smile.
- The individual is in a relationship that produces deflection structurally. For example, an individual in a potent identity who frequently becomes the object of another's actions will feel stressed by the depreciation of the potent identity.
- The individual cannot easily or quickly repair a distressing happening—like death of a loved one.

8.5.1 Self-Sentiments and Stress

Many individuals think of themselves as extremely nice, quite potent, and quite lively. If you are such a person, then you are not stressed when your friends, loved ones, and other valued individuals perform nice acts toward you. Extremely good events like becoming a parent or getting a promotion can be stressful, but not extremely stressful because the deflection from such events is limited—overly good impressions cannot be all that much more positive than what you want them to be. Having to interact with evil people would be emotionally unpleasant and would generate moderate to high levels of stress. However, the highest levels of stress arise when valued individuals treat you badly, thereby disconfirming sentiments about both you and the other. In other words, the worst stress results from good relationships going bad.

Individuals with negative selves run a general risk of seeming too nice—either because they are treated somewhat badly by others who dislike them, or because they are treated nicely by others who don't know about their negative self-concepts. In general, such individuals more often experience stress and its consequences than do individuals with positive selves.

8.5.2 Emotions and Stress

Deflection is related to unlikelihood: the more deflection an event produces, the stranger, more unique, even inconceivable the event seems. Thus life is stressful when it has turned persistently strange, unique, or inconceivable.

Deflection has no straightforward relation to emotion, and emotion is not an indicator of stress. Life can be intensely emotional and yet not stressful at all, when one is experiencing the emotions that are appropriate to one's identity. On the other hand, an emotionally flat life can be stressful for an individual who is trying to maintain a valued self.

For example, the joy and gleefulness of a mother playing with and chatting to her daughter are intense emotions, but they are close to the structural emotion for a mother with a daughter, and so frequent events of this sort produce little deflection and no stress. On the other hand, a mother catering to a sponging houseguest might feel no emotion as she repeatedly indulges the sponger, even as deflection is accruing and stress building. The stress is signaled by a sense that her life has turned unconventional, not by her lackluster feeling.

Any event that produces deflection can become stressful if repeated, and that includes events that produce pleasant emotions. For example, a fireman repeatedly acclaimed as a hero for acts of braveness is deflected in a positive direction, and if the accolades repeat over and over, a looming sense of peculiarity signals the growth of stress, even though the individual is feeling pride.

Events involving unpleasant emotions often produce great stress. That is not because negative emotions are inherently stressful, though. Rather, unpleasant emotions typically signal impressions of self that are far distant from the good, potent, and active self-sentiments that most people are trying to confirm, so the event producing unpleasant emotions also is producing massive deflection.

8.6 Emotions of Deviants

Clinical observations indicate that individuals with very negative self-esteem often have unstable emotions, or emotional lability. In fact, emotional lability should occur whenever an individual occupies a negatively evaluated identity (as does happen more often for those with negative self-esteem).

Think of a dissolute deviant, like a rapist. Imagine this individual grinning. Or imagine his face in an expression of woe. Such displays of emotion may strike you as insignificant in someone so bad, telling you little about his real assessments of things. The grin should signal that he is experiencing things as highly pleasant, but you doubt that because happiness is so inconsistent with his nature. The woeful attitude should signal that he is more tormented than usual, but you question that because wretchedness is so appropriate to his nature. Indeed, if the rapist thinks of himself as others do, he has to exaggerate his emotions in order to keep his self-feeling appropriate to his circumstances.

A simple smile or frown has little significance for individuals who understand themselves as being fundamentally bad. They have to be more demonstrative in order to experience somatically a small amount of deviation from their self-sentiment. When involved in social events producing overly positive impressions of themselves, they have to work themselves into emotional beatitude or euphoria in order to get to a somatic state that makes them feel as deflected from their negative identity as the external events make them seem. When involved in exceptionally negative events, they have to evoke emotional hell to obtain a somatic state that lets them experience themselves at the same levels of badness as the external events make them seem. Their emotions may swing from pleasant to unpleasant no more than others' do, but they have to emote more intensely to register the swings.

8.7 Further Readings

The decades-long research of psychologist Paul Ekman revolutionized thinking about emotion displays. An introduction to his work is available in his 2004 book *Emotions Revealed: Recognizing Faces and Feelings to Improve Communication and Emotional Life*.

The emotional dilemmas of flight attendants were analyzed in Arlie Hochschild's (1983) classic book in the sociology of emotions, *The Managed Heart: Commercialization of Human Feeling*. Another classic book in the sociology of emotions is T. David Kemper's (1978) *A Social Interactional Theory of Emotion*, which introduced the notion of structural emotions.

Some of the words referring to emotions in this chapter are not emotion words, strictly speaking. Andrew Ortony, Gerald Clore, and Mark Foss (1987) provided the definitive list in their article, "The referential structure of the affective lexicon."

Christine Averett and I developed the model of how impressions develop from emotion-identity combinations in an article that is included in the book *Analyzing Social Interaction* (Smith-Lovin and Heise 1988). Lisa Thomas (now Thomassen) and I replicated and extended the model in our article "Predicting impressions created by combinations of emotion and social identity" (Heise and Thomas 1989). A Japanese version of the model was developed by Herman Smith, Takanori Matsuno, and Shuuichirou Ike (2001).

I discussed the place of emotions in group solidarity in my essay "Conditions for Empathic Solidarity" (Heise 1998).

A selection of key articles on how experiences create stress is available in Thomas Holmes and Ella David, *Life Change, Life Events, and Illness* (1989). A control-theory approach to stress was developed by Raymond Pavloski (1989) in his chapter, "The physiological stress of thwarted intentions." Peggy Thoits emphasized intractability as a dimension of stress in her 1994 article, "Stressors and problem-solving: The individual as psychological activist." Linda Francis (1997) analyzed strategies for coping with partner loss in her article "Ideology and interpersonal emotion management: Redefining identity in two support groups."

9

Changing Sentiments

Individuals with comparable sentiments who share the same definition of a situation all have similar expectations about what should happen next. Thus their interaction generally proceeds routinely, each individual's action being anticipated by others. Even individuals' emotions are anticipated, seeming appropriate to their predicaments.

So behaviors and emotions that violate your expectations imply that others are not sharing your definition of the situation and your sentiments. One way to deal with that problem is to re-define the situation. If others seem to be affirming different identities than you supposed, then choose new identities for them that account for their conduct and emotions.

9.1 Re-Identification

You can re-identify an individual with an entirely new identity—that is the focus of labeling theory in sociology. Assigning a new identity amounts to accounting for the individual's recent actions in terms of revised role expectations. Alternatively, you can re-identify a person by combining a personal characteristic with the individual's current identity—that is the focus of trait attribution studies in psychology. Combining a trait modifier with the individual's original identity amounts to interpreting recent actions in terms of the individual's unique personality or character.

Suppose, for example, that you identify an individual as a doctor and her interaction partner as a patient, and you think that doctors are quite good and powerful and somewhat lively, and patients are a bit good, but weak and quiet. Now suppose you observe the doctor insulting the patient. That is not an act you expect. So how do you reconstruct the situation in order to understand this action better?

Redefining the doctor requires answering the question: What kind of person would insult a patient? The impression of a doctor who insults a patient is slightly bad, slightly potent, and slightly active, so you might try an identity with that affective meaning—e.g., critic. Such a re-identification works to a degree: a critic insulting a patient does maintain the meaning of patient and also confirms the potency and activity meanings of a critic. However, when the actor's identity is bad then the impression created by insulting is especially bad, so it's better to provide the actor with an even more negative identity, like quack. The impressions created by a quack insulting a patient are close to the sentiments for quacks and patients, so with this re-identification the event produces little deflection and seems plausible. The quack identity helps you understand the doctor's current behavior, and presumably it will help you understand her future behavior, too.

Alternatively, you can try to understand the insult as the act of a doctor with a peculiar character or personality. As just seen, an actor who insults a patient must be quite bad, somewhat potent, and slightly active. So what kind of a trait would make a doctor into such a person? The answer is, a trait that is quite bad, neutral on potency, and a bit lively—like inconsiderate. A doctor insulting a patient could be manifesting her general inconsiderateness. Henceforth you might use that trait to understand her peculiar behavior as a doctor, and her peculiar behavior in other roles, too.

Redefining the patient offers a different route to understanding the doctor's action. In this case, you ask the question: What kind of person would a doctor insult? The kind of person befitting insult from a doctor would be bad, weak, and a bit active. An alcoholic is one identity whose affective meaning is close to this profile. Thus, you could better understand the doctor's insult by viewing the recipient as an alcoholic instead of a patient, assuming that facts do not preclude this. Alternatively you could attribute a trait like self-centered or conceited to the patient. A self-centered, conceited patient plausibly befits a doctor's insult.

The example illustrates a general point. You re-identify participants in puzzling events so that outcome impressions are as close as possible to the sentiments provided by the new identifications. Events revised this way seem likely and no longer puzzling. You gain understanding of observed behaviors by choosing new identifications that minimize deflection.

9.1.1 Identity Filtering

Typically, there are many identities that would be affectively appropriate for an observed behavior. Some don't make sense because they conflict with the institutional setting in which the action occurred. For example, a doctor who insults a patient logically can be re-identified as a quack. However, the doctor cannot logically be re-identified as a burglar, traitor, or bigamist, even though these identities are just as affectively appropriate as quack. A re-identification has to stay true to the identity of the interaction partner, the setting, and the nature of the act performed.

A re-identification also has to accord with essential features of the person being re-identified—especially whether the individual is male or female. The women's movement has made gender less of an issue in the workplace, where many identities like executive, which were implicitly gendered, are becoming ungendered, and where explicitly gendered identities like chairman have been changed to ungendered forms (chair). However, appropriate use of gender still is important in labeling others with some informal identities such as beauty, stud, bitch, and bastard.

Individuals acquire institutionalized identities through ritual commissioning or by ascription from physical features (as in assigning son or daughter identities to newborns). Thus, casting an individual into an institutional identity beyond the one that is current in the situation almost always involves drawing on the individual's repertoire of established institutional identities. Considerable institutional work would be required to assign an institutional identity to someone who does not already have it.

Informal identities, like friend or foe, can be assigned more freely. The logical requirement is that the person is behaving in accordance with the identity, and the person's action does not seem to be confirming or repairing some other identity in his or her repertoire.

You stop using an informal identity when you cannot recollect an instance where the person did the kind of thing characteristic of that identity, as opposed to performing some other role. Thus, feeling embittered, you might withdraw the label of friend from a person after re-examining all your encounters and deciding that each of the other's friendly acts really had an ulterior motivation.

9.1.2 Labeling Deviants

Negatively evaluated identities are used to label deviants. Table 9-1 lists some sample identities that have negative evaluation, for males and females in the U.S.A.

Deviants who are weak range from quiet types to noisy types. As the perceived potency increases, however, deviants mostly are highly active.

Table 9-1 shows great variety in the kinds of deviants that exist. For instance, individuals may be deviants because of their social relations, expressive displays, appearance, use of money, means of gaining money, style of work participation, use of substances, mental ability, thought disorders, orientation to rules, trustworthiness, sexual behavior, or propensity to violence. Additionally there are labels to identify deviant youths, family deviants, supernatural deviants, judicial deviants, and those who are stigmatized because they are victims of others.

The diversity of deviants in most cells of the chart demonstrates that affectively appropriate labels might not all "fit the crime." You have to decide which affectively-appropriate label matches the functional significance of an individual's action. For example, you can't explain violent behavior by identifying someone as a safecracker (roughneck would make more sense), or sexual behavior by labeling someone as a vandal (instead of, say, an adulterer).

Something else to remember about labeling is that re-identifications need not occur in response to deviant actions. If your definition of the situation does not predict another's conduct or emotions, you generally try re-interpretation first, going back over actions and seeing if you understood everything correctly. Next you may try attributions about participants' personalities or moods. Only if none of this works are you forced to seek new identities for participants under the assumption that others are acting the way they do in order to confirm identities that you have not acknowledged.

Table 9-1. Some identities that were negatively evaluated in 1970s U.S.A.

	Inactive	Neutral	Active
Potent	stepfather*	mafioso ogre vampire witch	assassin bandit bouncer brute bully cutthroat fiend gangster gunman lady-killer loan-shark mobster pimp pusher racketeer rival roughneck safe-cracker tough vigilante villain
Neutral	miser scrooge tightwad	cynic glutton goon informer killjoy shrew sluggard snob snoop stuffed-shirt traitor wrongdoer	adulterer blabbermouth brat busybody criminal fanatic fugitive gambler gigolo gossip heel hooker hotshot lesbian pickpocket porno-star psychopath rat tease thief troublemaker vandal
Impotent	beggar coward crone deadbeat deadhead drudge dullard fuddy-duddy hag hermit hobo hypochondriac loafer shut-in wino zombie	captive clod degenerate dope drunkard faultfinder flunky halfwit homosexual hypocrite imbecile neurotic paranoid phony prisoner scapegoat sissy slave slob stoolpigeon sucker tramp weirdo windbag	bisexual braggart crybaby delinquent dropout drug-addict fink jackass jerk junkie lunatic peeping-tom pothead prostitute punk scatterbrain shoplifter sinner slut smart-aleck sorehead whore

* Stepfather is not a quiet identity for females, but it is close and gives a sense of what contents the cell could have with a larger sample of identities.

9.1.3 Attribution

An attribution amalgamates a modifier with an individual's identity. Making attributions can be a way of inferring an individual's personality traits. It also can be a way of inferring individuals' moods. Whether you infer a trait as opposed to a mood is essentially a logical matter.

Personality traits (like introverted or hostile) distinguish the manner in which an individual participates in a situation from the manner that is expected due to the individual's identity. Inferring a trait amounts to interpreting abnormal behavior in a situation as normal for that particular individual, because of the individual's personality.

Several conditions have to be fulfilled for a trait to be inferred. First, you have to notice an individual engaging in actions that disconfirm the individual's identity. Second, you have to note that the individual foregoes opportunities to repair the disconfirmation of identity, implying that the individual doesn't sense a problem. Since traits are trans-situational, a third condition also must be fulfilled: you are not aware of the individual acting elsewhere in a way that negates the inferred trait.

For example, suppose you visit someone who works in the same job as you but in a different establishment, and you observe the individual working in a manner that is low-keyed and taciturn relative to role demands, even in encounters that would excite you and make you talkative. You decide that the individual is introverted. However, that trait attribution could get scotched if you both go to a coffee house after work, and you see the individual visiting table after table, laughing and talking loudly with friends.

Mood attributions serve the same function as trait attributions, but moods do not have to be trans-situational. Inferring a mood requires that an individual acts abnormally relative to a role, and the abnormality continues even through opportunities to correct abnormal impressions. Disconfirmation of the mood in a different situation does not undermine the inference that the individual was in a mood previously.

Continuing the example, after seeing the individual's volubility after work, you conclude that the individual is not introverted but instead must have been in a heavy-hearted mood at work. You might even query the person to find out the reason for the moodiness earlier in the day.

9.1.4 Inferences From Emotionality

Sometimes people assess each other on the basis of conduct plus the emotional tone displayed while acting.

Malicious action accompanied by anguish damages an actor less than malicious action accompanied by satisfaction. The negative emotion signals that the actor actually is operating within a positive identity even though doing something bad. On the other hand, positive emotion during bad behavior implies that the actor is maintaining a negative identity, because only deviants engage in wicked behavior and feel good about it.

Such considerations become important in courtrooms. Defendants who show remorse about their illegal deeds get reduced punishments! They don't seem as inherently bad as defendants who show no remorse or who grin during accounts of their criminal acts.

Conversely, displaying negative emotion during positive actions leads to negative re-identifications. Imagine how you would classify someone who looks disgusted while kissing you! You expect others to have pleasant emotions when engaged in good actions, and something presumably is wrong with those who emote negatively while doing good.

Emotions displayed by recipients of action also can influence re-identifications of an actor. For example, you might suppose that a woman conversing warmly with a man is his friend, until you notice that the man is embarrassed. Then you might wonder if the woman is something grander, like a top executive, because smart, authoritative, or famous actors make others feel quiet, uncomfortable, and vulnerable! Thus the identity of an actor is linked to the expressed emotions of both the actor and the recipient of action.

If you have no information on participants' emotions during an action that instigates re-identification, then you ordinarily search for an identity to explain the action while assuming that the person is maintaining the characteristic emotion associated with that identity. Additionally you presume that the other person in the action also is experiencing the emotion characteristic of his or her identity.

9.1.5 Identity Fluctuation

People give up their definitions of a situation reluctantly, even to the point of endangering themselves at times. For example, scores of people died in a 1977 dinner-club fire in Kentucky because they interpreted an announcer's appeals to leave the room as just another comedic routine, rather than as warning of an emerging scene of horror and panic.

Yet definitions of social interactants are fluid, too, as you easily can prove by watching yourself to see how you turn others into grumps and jerks and other things, attribute moods and traits, and do all this with a flexibility that might take someone from hero to fool and back again within a few actions.

People seem to maintain multiple definitions of a situation: a stable proper one along with loose informal definitions. The proper definition of a situation doesn't change easily, and perhaps can't change easily because it is anchored in the material setting and weaved into participants' social networks at and beyond the scene. However, informal definitions, tacit and ephemeral, may last just as long as they are needed to explain occurring actions and emotions.

Arguments and betrayals wouldn't happen if people always maintained the positive identities of proper definitions: parents with children, co-professionals, co-workers, roommates, teammates—all can be only supportive with each other. Actors require negative identities to argue, exploit, nag, lie, abandon, ridicule, heckle, shun, etc. Since such negative actions occur, the implication is that people slip into negative identities without too much resistance. And most interpersonal turmoil is transitory, so returning to positive roles must be possible, too.

9.2 Sentiment Change

Most of the time you assimilate the world into your mental model, making your experiences fit your current knowledge and sentiments. You appraise situations in terms of concepts you know, and you construct and re-construct events so that they confirm the sentiments you have.

Yet at some points in life, you must change your mind, in order to keep a useful mental model that works reasonably well. Under what conditions does your mental model stop being a mold for shaping reality and instead adjust to reality?

9.2.1 New Sentiments

Events that are totally foreign to you cannot be assimilated into your existing mental model. You have to add concepts and their associated sentiments when you encounter an entirely new world of experience, a world for which you have no model at all.

Suppose, for example, that you turn to running rapids on the Colorado River for the first time in your life. Your guides provide you with concepts and sentiments for phenomena that you never encountered before. The river, your guides tell you, contains holes, stairs, sleepers, stoppers, keepers—phenomena that warrant your respect and perhaps your fear. You must learn life-saving responses to a boat flipping—swimming feet first, throwing bag, and participating in z-drags. River guides, you learn, are heroic figures warranting your respect as they scout whitewater ahead and thread your boat among dangerous rocks. Having acquired the mental model for river running, you must maintain it responsibly through your own actions, for the sake of everyone's safety.

Youths often are tabula rasa, lacking any model for an area of reality, and youths are expected to mentally incorporate whole spheres of culture. However, accommodation to reality occurs throughout life, whenever one moves into new vocational or avocational arenas.

9.2.2 Enculturation

Average high school graduates know about 50,000 words. For each word, they have learned a denotation and also the affective tone—or sentiment—associated with the concept. Thus individuals internalize a huge number of sentiments as they acquire language.

While some words and sentiments are learned via reading and dictionary usage, most sentiments associated with words are learned in interpersonal situations. Those who are more adept at a scene convey sentiments to novices directly by emotional displays, or indirectly by actions.

For example, apprentice builders might learn the sentiment for building inspectors by observing their employers' nervousness when interacting with building inspectors. Alternatively, they might surmise the appropriate sentiment toward building inspectors from a building inspector's actions, like halting a construction project until violations of the building code have been remedied.

9.2.3 Turning Points

Occasionally some event prompts a need to adjust your sentiments, and you deliberately open yourself to sentiment change.

Suppose, for example, that a male acquaintance leading a dissipated life falls in love and marries. Guessing that your old sentiment about him may no longer be predictive of his future actions, you open your mind and let his subsequent actions shape a new sentiment that allows you to generate reasonable expectations about his future behavior.

Catastrophes that leave individuals unable to anticipate the events in their lives can open them to replacement of major portions of their mental models. Religious missionaries make use of this fact, entering disaster areas and generating orderliness through implementation of their religion's conceptualizations and sentiments. Seeing the power of the missionaries' mental models and the inadequacy of their old culture, indigens may abandon in mass their old cultural understandings for the new doctrines offered by the missionaries.

Accommodation occurs when you are not entirely in control of life, implying some impotency, and successful accommodation may even require temporary forfeiting of potency in order to change. Formal accommodation roles—like apprentice, beginner, intern, trainee, and the roles of childhood—all have a pattern of being nice but somewhat powerless.

Having gone into the mode of accommodating to reality with regard to some entity, you stay in that mode as long as your surmised sentiment for the entity keeps changing. However, when you surmise the same sentiment over and over—say, four or five times, you switch from accommodator to assimilator mode, and begin constructing and re-constructing events so as to confirm your stable sentiment.

9.3 Further Readings

Books on affect control theory (Heise 1979; Smith-Lovin and Heise 1988; MacKinnon 1994) discuss re-identification in detail.

The importance of emotional demeanor in courtrooms has been investigated in a series of studies by Olga Tsoudis, Lynn Smith-Lovin, and Dawn Robinson (Robinson, Smith-Lovin, and Tsoudis 1994; Tsoudis and Smith-Lovin 1998; 2001; Tsoudis 2000a; 2000b;).

Psychologist Jean Piaget developed the idea of assimilation versus accommodation—e.g., see his 1954 book, *The Construction of Reality in the Child*. I applied the idea in an article on how sentiments accommodate to events: "Sentiment formation in social interaction" (Heise 2006).

The estimate of vocabulary acquisition comes from George A. Miller (1991), *The Science of Words*.

I examined the impact of catastrophes on religious conversion in my 1967 article, "Prefatory findings in the sociology of missions."

My knowledge of white-water boating comes entirely from Lilian Jonas (1999), "Making and facing danger: Constructing strong character on the river."

10

Selves

Just as you select behaviors to confirm the identity you occupy at the moment, you impart your self-meaning to yourself and others by enacting identities whose sentiments convey your sentiment about yourself.

For example, if you are a woman who feels that you are very good, potent, and very lively—a common self-sentiment of young middle class females in Canada and the U.S.A.—then you are actualized mainly by family and romantic identities and by some informal identities relating to friendship and vivacity. If you are a man who feels that you are somewhat good while being potent, and very lively—common among young middle class males in Canada and the U.S.A.—then you are actualized by family and romantic identities and by informal identities relating to friendship and extroversion, but additionally, since you maintain a less elevated self-esteem than females, you can self-actualize in student roles and in jobs that involve working crowds, like bartender.

Expressing your self-sentiment through identities gives you a personal agenda when defining a situation. For example, the females mentioned above will prefer to define situations in terms of identities for family, romance, friendship, or sociability—even when they are in school and occupational settings. The males mentioned above would have similar preferences, except additionally the males easily could define some situations in terms of identities for education or occupation.

Of course, definitions of situations are not determined by personal preferences alone. Physical realities can force situational definitions, as when a disaster turns everyone into victims, helpers, or exploiters. Subordination, such as employment in a firm or enrollment in a course, leads to the imposition of a power-holder's definitions. Consequently, individuals sometimes must occupy inauthentic identities that fail to surrogate their self-sentiments.

You can absolve inauthenticity that results from enacting a required identity by later enacting another identity that diverges from the self-sentiment oppositely. In essence, you actualize your self-sentiment cumulatively. Though neither identity is directly self-actualizing, in combination they sustain and convey your self-sentiment.

For example, suppose that a middle-class Canadian male took a job as a musician. The identity of musician is insufficiently potent and active to actualize his self-sentiment, so time at work would create a sense of personal inauthenticity. However, the individual could redeem the self by pairing the musician identity with identities that are overly potent and active relative to the individual's self-sentiment—identities such as athlete and teammate. Thus the individual's schedule might alternate working as a musician with participation in team sports. The combination of identities actualizes the individual's self-sentiment, even though none of the identities is self-actualizing by itself.

10.1 Salient Identities

Identities that you can occupy change as you move from one institutional setting to another. Family situations require you to take an offspring, sibling, parental, nepotic, or avuncular identity. In academic situations, you can take student identities, or academician or alumni identities, if you are eligible for them. At a store you take a customer identity, or some kind of commercial identity if you work at the store. In a religious setting, you have a congregational identity, or a ministerial identity, or a visitor identity.

Some identities that you can take in an institutional setting may actualize your self-sentiment better than others. For example, as an adult at a family gathering, you may find your sibling identity more comfortable than your offspring identity, because your offspring identity can involve you in parental actions that diminish your potency, requiring you to undo the diminishment later by enacting some potent identity.

In effect, you rank identities in terms of how well they actualize your self-sentiment, separately for each social institution in which you spend time. As you move into a new institutional setting, your most self-actualizing identities in that institution are especially salient as a basis for defining your situation.

At least that is the case if you are not trying to redeem yourself from some prior inauthenticity. An unresolved prior inauthenticity changes the salience hierarchy of identities in an institution. For example, if you attend a family gathering soon after completing some daring action that earned you a near-heroic identity in another setting, you may prefer the offspring identity, in order to expunge your excess potency.

Incidentally, identities that match your self-sentiment but that you are not qualified to occupy, like an occupation requiring training that you have not had, still can be salient for you, as aspirations that you would like to achieve, or simply as roles with which you empathize. Like identities available to you, your aspirations and empathies change, depending on inauthenticities that you recently experienced.

10.1.1 Commitment and Alienation

An institution where you can self-actualize, or absolve inauthenticities acquired elsewhere, constitutes a rewarding environment for you. With freedom to choose, you commit more of your time to institutions of this kind than to institutions where you feel inauthentic in your roles.

Conversely, an institution in which you are forced to enact identities far from your self-concept is stressful, and, you can end up alienated by the whole institution if it gives you no opportunities for self-actualization. Then, with freedom to choose, you avoid the people and settings of the institution as much as possible. For example, some individuals are likely to be alienated from the legal institution after being processed for an offense like participation in a political protest. The identities of defendant and jail inmate are too far from their self-sentiments to want a repeat of the experience!

10.2 Deviance Forays

Very high self-esteem prevents individuals from occupying identities that are excessively positive for them, because their self-sentiment is close to the point where more positively evaluated identities cease to exist. Thus such individuals cannot experience inauthenticity from being overly valued, and lacking that kind of inauthenticity they do not have to redeem themselves in less valued identities.

However, individuals with more modest levels of self-esteem can get into predicaments of seeming excessively beneficent and wholesome, relative to their evaluation of self. Then they must occupy less valued identities to redeem themselves from the inauthenticity of excessive goodness. For example, some males experience inauthenticity when they take the identities of sweetheart or truelove. The faithfulness involved in such identities implies more wholesomeness than their self-esteem warrants, and they are apt to correct the imbalance later by occupying identities of duplicity—for instance, by being a sharpie or a pickup!

Inauthenticity of excessive goodness causes deviance as the individual balances one identity with another in order to actualize the self cumulatively. Thus the perplexing phenomenon of seemingly noble individuals "shooting themselves in the foot" with forays into misconduct arises from their having positive self-evaluations, but low enough self-evaluations to feel inauthentic during their finest hours. People with moderate self-esteem are positioned to take exalted identities, but they also can take degraded identities, and they are fated to take both once they take either.

10.3 Deviants

Most people have positive self-sentiments. However, some people lack self-esteem. For example, ordinary sociopaths rate themselves as neither good nor bad, as weak, and as lively. This kind of self-sentiment centers them among marginal and stigmatized identities, which they adopt for self-actualization, and as redemptions when they experience the inauthenticity of excessive goodness. Such identity preferences explain much of their behavior.

A sociopath's self-sentiment is close to the sentiments for boarder, migrant, runaway, and exile—all identities that relate to the itinerancy that is characteristic of sociopaths. The nearness of their self-sentiment to work identities like bootblack, gas station attendant, photographer, street musician, and taxi driver explains their prevalence in low-supervision, low-status jobs. Their marriage problems link to being close to identities like brute and shrew, plus the identities of divorcé or divorcée. Their polymorphic sexual behavior derives from the closeness of their self-sentiments to sentiments about the identities of bisexuality, homosexuality, promiscuity, and prostitution. Their high arrest rate befits their closeness to numerous identities of criminality and culpability. Their substance abuse problems correspond to being close to such identities as lush, drunk, pothead, and drug addict. Their multifarious psychiatric status fits their closeness to a number of mental-disorder identities like neurotic, lunatic, paranoid, and psychotic.

Thus, sociopaths' lack of self-esteem leads them to deviant identities, which in turn foster disapproved behavior and unpleasant life experiences.

10.3.1 Self-Repugnance

A small proportion of individuals actually disesteem themselves so much that they have to actualize themselves in identities that are socially condemned. Self-loathing individuals use culturally disvalued identities to embody their self-repugnance and convey that self-repugnance to themselves and others.

Self-loathing derives from victimization in the past. However, self-loathing individuals enact the destructive behaviors that confirm atrocious identities, thereby victimizing people in the present. Thereby self-repugnance regenerates itself from traumatized victim to traumatized victim.

The most dangerous individuals are those who drastically disesteem themselves while maintaining a sense of dominance and activity. Their self-sentiments access many of the sexuality, criminality, and mental-disorder identities mentioned for sociopaths, but push further into viciousness. For example, a self-sentiment of bad, potent, and active accesses informal identities like ruffian, heel, weirdo, rowdy, thug, rat, scoundrel, and hothead. The self-sentiment also can surrogate itself in identities of violent criminality like firebug, cutthroat, gunman, and murderer.

Notwithstanding its malignancy, a bad-strong-active self-sentiment also offers access to some workaday identities in normal society. For example, an individual with this kind of self-sentiment could tolerate the jobs of salesman, bill collector, real estate agent, truck driver, or construction laborer. For a self-loathing individual, though, the more acceptable the job, the greater the inauthenticity, so such work feeds urges to engage in compensatory deviance.

10.3.2 Patterns of Deviance

Self-repugnance alone does not guarantee viciousness. Self-repugnance can combine with various patterns of potency and activity to produce different types of deviant individuals. For example, a sense of self-loathing, impotency and inactivity disposes an individual to take on identities like drop-out, failure, flunky, has-been, loser, or nobody. The cells in Table 9-1 can be examined to get an idea of what identities accompany self-repugnance in combination with different patterns of potency and activity.

10.4 Self-Fluctuation

Self-esteem varies over the life course. On the average, self-evaluation is positive in childhood, takes a pronounced dip during adolescence, returns to quite positive values in adulthood, and gradually rises to a peak during the sixth or seventh decade of life, before plunging because of loss of health, mobility, and social relationships.

Few studies have examined life-long changes in the potency and activity of self. Available empirical evidence indicates only that self-potency is substantial but gradually declining at late mid-life.

Extrapolating the potency and activity of age-graded identities like child, adolescent, adult, and elder yields the following plausible patterns. Potency of the self might be low during childhood, then grow steadily up to mid-life, then decline gradually into old age, until infirmities cause a precipitous drop. Activity of the self might be high in childhood and peak during adolescence and early adulthood, then remain high through mid-life, and decline during old age.

If these speculations about life-course changes in self-sentiments are right, then the following forms of self-actualization would emerge at each stage of life, on the average.

- Childhood: self-actualization through the identities of childhood, with little interest in institutions that provide no childhood identities.
- Adolescence: self-actualization through informal identities related to games and competitions; aspirations to managerial jobs; interest in military roles; interest in identities of fortuitous sexuality (e.g., pick-up).
- Early adulthood: self-actualization through socializing and sports-related identities; aspirations to managerial positions but also interest in good jobs of modest nature; interest in military and patriotic roles; emerging interest in some religious identities; interest in sibling and spousal roles.
- Middle adulthood: self-actualization through exemplar identities (e.g., role model) and integrative roles in business; plus sibling, spousal, and parental identities; plus romantic identities of deep intimacy; expanded interest in religion.
- Late adulthood and early old age: self-actualization through identities of political participation; tutelage identities; empathy with healers; grandparent identity; romantic identities of deep intimacy.
- Final decline: self-actualization through identities of withdrawal and disability like medical patient and mourner.

10.4.1 Cultural Shifts in Self

Shifts in self-actualizing identities arise from a changing self-sentiment, and also from cultural changes in identity sentiments.

Consider the identity of smoker. Movies from the mid-twentieth century present smokers as sophisticated, so the identity's sentiment at that time presumably was like a sophisticate—slightly good, potent, and a bit active. Such an identity would have been a self-actualizing identity for some adolescents and young adults. However, by the turn of the twenty-first century the smoker sentiment had become very bad, impotent, and inactive. Thus the smoker identity is not self-actualizing for most people today, and those who sustain the smoker identity must redeem themselves by also maintaining positive compensating identities.

Cultural changes in sentiments about identities ordinarily occur over a period of decades, so the impact of cultural change is confounded with individuals' life course changes in self-sentiments. An individual's social character may change either because of a maturing self-sentiment or because of cultural shifts in identity sentiments.

Cultural changes produce contrasts between earlier and later cohorts, assuming that the average self-sentiments within age levels stay the same over time. For example, sophisticated young adults in the early 21st Century actualize themselves with different identities than young sophisticates in the mid-20th Century—smoker is out, body modifier is in!

10.5 Further Readings

The model of self presented in this chapter is from a book being written by Neil MacKinnon and myself, *Identities, Selves, and Social Institutions*. The relation of deviance to the self-sentiment also is developed in that book.

Self-actualization is a concept developed by Carl Rogers (1961) in *On Becoming a Person; A Therapist's View of Psychotherapy*. However, Rogers did not relate self-actualization to identities.

Self-sentiments of sociopaths were analyzed by Isaac Marks in his 1965 book *Patterns of Meaning in Psychiatric Patients: Semantic Differential Responses in Obsessives and Psychopaths*. Sociopathic behavior was analyzed by Lee Robins (1966) in her classic book *Deviant Children Grown Up: A Sociological and Psychiatric Study of Sociopathic Personality*.

David Demo's 1992 essay, "The self-concept over time: Research issues and directions," reviewed available research on self-esteem over the life course. A project by Richard Robins, Kali Trzesniewski, Jessica Tracy, Samuel Gosling, and Jeff Potter obtained self-esteem data from more than 300,000 individuals via the Internet, as reported in their 2002 article, "Global self-esteem across the life span." Robert Schafer and Pat Keith (1999) studied self-esteem over time, as reported in their article "Change in adult self-esteem: A longitudinal assessment."

Part 2

Mathematics of Affect Control Theory

11

Event Likelihood

In affect control theory, a deflection, D, measures the extent to which conditions generated by an event differ from past experience, as represented in the following schematic definition.

$$D: \begin{array}{c} \text{absolute} \\ \text{difference} \end{array} \left(\left\{ \begin{array}{c} \text{Historically} \\ \text{Anchored} \\ \text{State} \end{array} \right\} - \left\{ \begin{array}{c} \text{Event} \\ \text{Generated} \\ \text{State} \end{array} \right\} \right) \tag{11.1}$$

Since absolute values are troublesome in analysis, this conception is revised to

$$D: \left(\left\{ \begin{array}{c} \text{Historically} \\ \text{Anchored} \\ \text{State} \end{array} \right\} - \left\{ \begin{array}{c} \text{Event} \\ \text{Generated} \\ \text{State} \end{array} \right\} \right)^2 \tag{11.2}$$

and more specifically to

$$D_i = \left(f_i - \tau_i \right)^2 \tag{11.3}$$

where f represents a fundamental sentiment established in a personal or cultural history, and τ represents a transient impression that exists as a result of an event. The subscript, i, indicates that the sentiments, impressions, and deflections in an event have a number of different aspects.

The subjective likelihood, L, of an event is defined by the formula

$$L = c - \sum_{i=A_e}^{O_a} w_i D_i \qquad (11.4)$$

where c is an arbitrary constant, w stands for summation weights, and D_i are deflections for actor (A), behavior (B), and object (O) on the response dimensions of evaluation (e), potency (p), and activity (a). That is, i indexes over A_e, A_p, A_a, B_e, B_p, B_a, O_e, O_p, O_a (and also over S_e, S_p, S_a when settings are being considered).

Equation (11.4) means that an event seems more likely when it generates smaller deflections. Alternatively an event seems more unlikely (U), uncanny, or unique as deflections are larger—a proposition that has been verified empirically (Heise and MacKinnon 1987). This interpretation corresponds to the following equation.

$$U = k + \sum_{i=A_e}^{O_a} w_i D_i \qquad (11.5)$$

or, from equation (11.3),

$$U = k + \sum_{i=A_e}^{O_a} w_i \left(f_i - t_i \right)^2 \qquad (11.6)$$

or, writing out the terms in the summation and expanding the squares,

$$U = k + \left(w_{A_e} \overline{A}_e^2 - 2 w_{A_e} \overline{A}_e \hat{A}_e + w_{A_e} \hat{A}_e^2 \right) + \cdots \\ + \left(w_{O_a} \overline{O}_a^2 - 2 w_{O_a} \overline{O}_a \hat{O}_a + w_{O_a} \hat{O}_a^2 \right) \qquad (11.7)$$

where an over-line signifies measurement of a fundamental, and a caret signifies measurement of a post-event transient.

All fundamentals can be collected in a vector,

$$\mathbf{f}' = \left(\overline{A}_e \quad \overline{A}_p \quad \overline{A}_a \quad \overline{B}_e \quad \overline{B}_p \quad \overline{B}_a \quad \overline{O}_e \quad \overline{O}_p \quad \overline{O}_a \right) \qquad (11.8)$$

and all post-event transients in another vector,

$$\boldsymbol{\tau}' = \left(\hat{A}_e \quad \hat{A}_p \quad \hat{A}_a \quad \hat{B}_e \quad \hat{B}_p \quad \hat{B}_a \quad \hat{O}_e \quad \hat{O}_p \quad \hat{O}_a \right) \qquad (11.9)$$

and the weights can be organized in a diagonal matrix,

$$\mathbf{w} = \begin{pmatrix} w_{A_e} & 0 & 0 & 0 & 0 & 0 & 0 & 0 & 0 \\ 0 & w_{A_p} & 0 & 0 & 0 & 0 & 0 & 0 & 0 \\ 0 & 0 & w_{A_a} & 0 & 0 & 0 & 0 & 0 & 0 \\ 0 & 0 & 0 & w_{B_e} & 0 & 0 & 0 & 0 & 0 \\ 0 & 0 & 0 & 0 & w_{B_p} & 0 & 0 & 0 & 0 \\ 0 & 0 & 0 & 0 & 0 & w_{B_a} & 0 & 0 & 0 \\ 0 & 0 & 0 & 0 & 0 & 0 & w_{O_e} & 0 & 0 \\ 0 & 0 & 0 & 0 & 0 & 0 & 0 & w_{O_p} & 0 \\ 0 & 0 & 0 & 0 & 0 & 0 & 0 & 0 & w_{O_a} \end{pmatrix} \tag{11.10}$$

whereupon Eq. (11.6) becomes

$$U = k + \begin{pmatrix} \mathbf{f}' & \boldsymbol{\tau}' \end{pmatrix} \begin{pmatrix} \mathbf{W} & -\mathbf{W} \\ -\mathbf{W} & \mathbf{W} \end{pmatrix} \begin{pmatrix} \mathbf{f} \\ \boldsymbol{\tau} \end{pmatrix} \tag{11.11}$$

If weights for all terms are equal to 1.0 (and this presumption has been found adequate for simulations of social interaction—Heise 1985a) then $\mathbf{W}$ is an identity matrix, and Eq. (11.11) becomes

$$U = k + \begin{pmatrix} \mathbf{f}' & \boldsymbol{\tau}' \end{pmatrix} \begin{pmatrix} \mathbf{I} & -\mathbf{I} \\ -\mathbf{I} & \mathbf{I} \end{pmatrix} \begin{pmatrix} \mathbf{f} \\ \boldsymbol{\tau} \end{pmatrix} \tag{11.12}$$

On the other hand, in principle, weights might differ from term to term for fundamentals, transients, and cross-products, in which case the summation still is a quadratic form, but not necessarily the one corresponding to squared differences, shown in Eq. (11.7). This generalization is incorporated because it relates to a later derivation.

$$U = k + \begin{pmatrix} \mathbf{f}' & \boldsymbol{\tau}' \end{pmatrix} \begin{pmatrix} \mathbf{W}_{ff} & -\mathbf{W}_{f\tau} \\ -\mathbf{W}_{f\tau} & \mathbf{W}_{\tau\tau} \end{pmatrix} \begin{pmatrix} \mathbf{f} \\ \boldsymbol{\tau} \end{pmatrix} \tag{11.13}$$

Indeed, at this point it is easy to generalize the quadratic form further by including first-order terms:

$$U = k + \begin{pmatrix} \mathbf{f}' & \boldsymbol{\tau}' \end{pmatrix} \begin{pmatrix} \mathbf{W}_{ff} & -\mathbf{W}_{f\tau} \\ -\mathbf{W}_{f\tau} & \mathbf{W}_{\tau\tau} \end{pmatrix} \begin{pmatrix} \mathbf{f} \\ \boldsymbol{\tau} \end{pmatrix} + \begin{pmatrix} \mathbf{v}_f' & \mathbf{v}_\tau' \end{pmatrix} \begin{pmatrix} \mathbf{f} \\ \boldsymbol{\tau} \end{pmatrix} \tag{11.14}$$

where $\mathbf{v}_f$ and $\mathbf{v}_\tau$ each is a vector of weights. The notion is that a sense of unlikeliness might spring directly from some of sentiments involved in an event or from some of the impressions produced by an event, as well as from comparing impressions with sentiments.

The transients existing after an event can be predicted from the transients that precede the event (Smith-Lovin 1987b):

$$\tau = \mathbf{M}'\mathbf{t} \tag{11.15}$$

$\mathbf{M}$ is the matrix of prediction coefficients estimated in impression-formation research, with one column for each post-event transient being predicted. Vector $\mathbf{t}$ contains pre-event transients along with interaction terms that have been found to have predictive value in empirical analyses.

The following composition of $\mathbf{t}$ follows the report of Smith-Lovin (1987b); this composition was used in simulations created with versions of computer program *Interact* distributed prior to 1991.

$$
\begin{aligned}
\mathbf{t}' = (1 \quad & A_e \quad A_p \quad A_a \quad B_e \quad B_p \quad B_a \quad O_e \quad O_p \quad O_a \\
& A_e B_e \quad A_e B_p \quad A_e B_a \quad A_p B_e \quad A_p B_p \quad A_p O_a \quad A_a B_a \\
& B_e O_e \quad B_e O_p \quad B_p O_e \quad B_p O_p \quad B_p O_a \quad B_a O_e \quad B_a O_p \\
& A_e B_e O_e \quad A_e B_p O_p \quad A_p B_p O_p \quad A_p B_p O_a \quad A_a B_a O_a)
\end{aligned}
\tag{11.16}
$$

Specification of interactions for predicting affective outcomes can vary depending on equation estimation procedures. Smith-Lovin inferred the above during her maximum-likelihood estimations of impression-formation equations. A different specification obtained with least-squares procedures applied to the same data will be offered in Eq. (12.24). Additionally, it is an open issue whether specification of interactions varies across cultures, though the issue has been addressed for Japan versus the U.S.A. (Smith, Matsuno, and Umino 1994).

Substituting the value of tau given in Eq. (11.15), Eq. (11.14) becomes:

$$
U = k + \begin{pmatrix} \mathbf{f}' & \mathbf{t}'\mathbf{M} \end{pmatrix}
\begin{pmatrix} \mathbf{W}_{ff} & -\mathbf{W}_{f\tau} \\ -\mathbf{W}_{f\tau} & \mathbf{W}_{\tau\tau} \end{pmatrix}
\begin{pmatrix} \mathbf{f} \\ \mathbf{M}'\mathbf{t} \end{pmatrix}
+ \begin{pmatrix} \mathbf{v}_f' & \mathbf{v}_\tau' \end{pmatrix}
\begin{pmatrix} \mathbf{f} \\ \mathbf{M}'\mathbf{t} \end{pmatrix}
\tag{11.17}
$$

Terms involving pre-existing transients now can be isolated in a vector along with the fundamentals as follows.

$$
U = k + \begin{pmatrix} \mathbf{f}' & \mathbf{t}' \end{pmatrix}
\begin{pmatrix} \mathbf{W}_{ff} & -\mathbf{W}_{f\tau}\mathbf{M}' \\ -\mathbf{M}\mathbf{W}_{f\tau} & \mathbf{M}\mathbf{W}_{\tau\tau}\mathbf{M}' \end{pmatrix}
\begin{pmatrix} \mathbf{f} \\ \mathbf{t} \end{pmatrix}
+ \begin{pmatrix} \mathbf{v}_f' & \mathbf{v}_\tau'\mathbf{M} \end{pmatrix}
\begin{pmatrix} \mathbf{f} \\ \mathbf{t} \end{pmatrix}
\tag{11.18}
$$

Equation (11.18) indicates that the unlikeliness-uncanniness-uniqueness of a specified future event can be determined entirely in terms of quantities that exist before the event occurs, namely, cultural definitions ($\mathbf{f}$), parameters describing psychological processes ($\mathbf{M}$, $\mathbf{W}$, and $\mathbf{V}$), and circumstances produced by recent events ($\mathbf{t}$).

12

Optimal Behavior

The evaluation-potency-activity profile for the behavior that would minimize unlike-liness-uncanniness-uniqueness and maximize normality is obtained by setting partial derivatives of the right side of Eq. (11.18) to zero and solving for behavior terms. Before doing this, though, the behavior variables in $(\mathbf{f'\ t'})$ must be removed to a separate vector. This is accomplished by defining $\mathbf{z}_\beta$, a vector that draws out the behavior terms in $(\mathbf{f'\ t'})$ and which has ones corresponding to entries in $(\mathbf{f'\ t'})$ that lack a behavior term.

$$
\begin{aligned}
\mathbf{z}'_\beta = (1 \quad 1 \quad 1 \quad & \bar{B}_e \quad \bar{B}_p \quad \bar{B}_a \quad 1 \quad 1 \quad 1 \\
1 \quad 1 \quad 1 \quad 1 \quad & \bar{B}_e \quad \bar{B}_p \quad \bar{B}_a \quad 1 \quad 1 \quad 1 \\
\bar{B}_e \quad \bar{B}_p \quad \bar{B}_a \quad & \bar{B}_e \quad \bar{B}_p \quad 1 \quad \bar{B}_a \\
\bar{B}_e \quad \bar{B}_e \quad \bar{B}_p \quad & \bar{B}_p \quad \bar{B}_p \quad \bar{B}_a \quad \bar{B}_a \\
\bar{B}_e \quad \bar{B}_p \quad & \bar{B}_p \quad \bar{B}_p \quad \bar{B}_a)
\end{aligned}
\tag{12.1}
$$

Assuming that behaviors are recalled from memory with transients set equal to fundamental values, this becomes

$$
\begin{aligned}
\mathbf{z}'_\beta = (1 \quad 1 \quad 1 \quad & \bar{B}_e \quad \bar{B}_p \quad \bar{B}_a \quad 1 \quad 1 \quad 1 \\
1 \quad 1 \quad 1 \quad 1 \quad & \bar{B}_e \quad \bar{B}_p \quad \bar{B}_a \quad 1 \quad 1 \quad 1 \\
\bar{B}_e \quad \bar{B}_p \quad \bar{B}_a \quad & \bar{B}_e \quad \bar{B}_p \quad 1 \quad \bar{B}_a \\
\bar{B}_e \quad \bar{B}_e \quad \bar{B}_p \quad & \bar{B}_p \quad \bar{B}_p \quad \bar{B}_a \quad \bar{B}_a \\
\bar{B}_e \quad \bar{B}_p \quad & \bar{B}_p \quad \bar{B}_p \quad \bar{B}_a)
\end{aligned}
\tag{12.2}
$$

A diagonal matrix, $\mathbf{I}_\beta$, also is defined to contain elements of $(\mathbf{f}'\ \mathbf{t}')$ that were not moved to $\mathbf{z}_\beta$.

$$\text{Diagonal } \mathbf{I}_\beta = (\bar{A}_e \quad \bar{A}_p \quad \bar{A}_a \quad 1 \quad 1 \quad 1 \quad \bar{O}_e \quad \bar{O}_p \quad \bar{O}_a$$

$$1 \quad A_e \quad A_p \quad A_a \quad 1 \quad 1 \quad 1 \quad O_e \quad O_p \quad O_a$$

$$A_e \quad A_e \quad A_e \quad A_p \quad A_p \quad A_p O_a \quad A_a \tag{12.3}$$

$$O_e \quad O_p \quad O_e \quad O_p \quad O_a \quad O_e \quad O_p$$

$$A_e O_e \quad A_e O_p \quad A_p O_p \quad A_p O_a \quad A_a O_a)$$

Now $(\mathbf{f}'\ \mathbf{t}')$ can be expressed as

$$(\mathbf{f}'\ \mathbf{t}') = \mathbf{z}'_\beta \mathbf{I}_\beta \tag{12.4}$$

and Eq. (11.18) as

$$U = k + \mathbf{z}'_\beta \mathbf{I}_\beta \begin{pmatrix} \mathbf{W}_{ff} & -\mathbf{W}_{fr}\mathbf{M}' \\ -\mathbf{M}\mathbf{W}_{fr} & \mathbf{M}\mathbf{W}_{\tau\tau}\mathbf{M}' \end{pmatrix} \mathbf{I}_\beta \mathbf{z}_\beta + (\mathbf{v}'_f \quad \mathbf{v}'_\tau \mathbf{M}) \mathbf{I}_\beta \mathbf{z}_\beta \tag{12.5}$$

At this point a behavior profile

$$\mathbf{b}' = (\bar{B}_e \quad \bar{B}_p \quad \bar{B}_a) \tag{12.6}$$

can be obtained from $\mathbf{z}_\beta$ by defining a selection matrix:

$$\mathbf{S}'_\beta = \begin{pmatrix}
0 & 0 & 0 & 1 & 0 & 0 & 0 & 0 & 0 & 0 & 0 & 0 & 0 \\
0 & 0 & 0 & 0 & 1 & 0 & 0 & 0 & 0 & 0 & 0 & 0 & 0 \\
0 & 0 & 0 & 0 & 0 & 1 & 0 & 0 & 0 & 0 & 0 & 0 & 0 \\
1 & 0 & 0 & 0 & 0 & 0 & 1 & 0 & 0 & 1 & 0 & 0 & 0 \\
0 & 1 & 0 & 0 & 0 & 0 & 0 & 1 & 0 & 0 & 1 & 0 & 0 \\
0 & 0 & 1 & 0 & 0 & 0 & 0 & 0 & 1 & 0 & 0 & 0 & 1 \\
1 & 1 & 0 & 0 & 0 & 0 & 0 & 1 & 0 & 0 & 0 & 0 & 0 \\
0 & 0 & 1 & 1 & 1 & 0 & 0 & 0 & 1 & 1 & 1 & 0 \\
0 & 0 & 0 & 0 & 0 & 1 & 1 & 0 & 0 & 0 & 0 & 1
\end{pmatrix} \tag{12.7}$$

Ones in the first row of Eq. (12.7) show where $\bar{B}_e$ terms arise in $\mathbf{z}_\beta$, ones in the second row designate $\bar{B}_p$ terms, and ones in the third row show $\bar{B}_a$ terms. The product, $\mathbf{S}'\mathbf{b}$, reconstructs $\mathbf{z}_\beta$ except that there are zeros where ones should be. Thus another vector of zeros and ones is defined—a vector in which ones show the terms of $(\mathbf{f}'\ \mathbf{t}')$ that lack any behavior term. This can be obtained from the selection matrix as follows.

$$\mathbf{g} = \mathbf{1}_S - \mathbf{S}_\beta \mathbf{1}_3 \tag{12.8}$$

Where $\mathbf{1}_S$ is a vector of ones with the same row order as $\mathbf{S}_\beta$, and $\mathbf{1}_3$ is a vector of three ones. In the particular case being considered:

$$\mathbf{g}'_\beta = (1\ \ 1\ \ 1\ \ 0\ \ 0\ \ 0\ \ 1\ \ 1\ \ 1\ \ 1\ \ 1\ \ 1\ \ 1$$
$$0\ \ 0\ \ 0\ \ 1\ \ 1\ \ 1\ \ 0\ \ 0\ \ 0\ \ 0\ \ 0\ \ 1\ \ 0 \tag{12.9}$$
$$0\ \ 0\ \ 0\ \ 0\ \ 0\ \ 0\ \ 0\ \ 0\ \ 0\ \ 0\ \ 0\ \ 0)$$

Then

$$\mathbf{z}'_\beta = \mathbf{g}'_\beta + \mathbf{b}'\mathbf{S}'_\beta \tag{12.10}$$

Using Eq. (12.10) the equation for unlikeliness-uncanniness-uniqueness can be expressed with the behavior profile explicit

$$U = k + \left(\mathbf{g}'_\beta + \mathbf{b}'\mathbf{S}'_\beta\right)\mathbf{I}_\beta \begin{pmatrix} \mathbf{W}_{ff} & -\mathbf{W}_{f\tau}\mathbf{M}' \\ -\mathbf{M}\mathbf{W}_{f\tau} & \mathbf{M}\mathbf{W}_{\tau\tau}\mathbf{M}' \end{pmatrix} \mathbf{I}_\beta \left(\mathbf{g}_\beta + \mathbf{S}_\beta \mathbf{b}\right)$$
$$+ \left(\mathbf{v}'_f\ \ \mathbf{v}'_\tau \mathbf{M}\right)\mathbf{I}_\beta \left(\mathbf{g}_\beta + \mathbf{S}_\beta \mathbf{b}\right) \tag{12.11}$$

For convenience, symbolize the matrices of constant parameters

$$\mathbf{H} = \begin{pmatrix} \mathbf{W}_{ff} & -\mathbf{W}_{f\tau}\mathbf{M}' \\ -\mathbf{M}\mathbf{W}_{f\tau} & \mathbf{M}\mathbf{W}_{\tau\tau}\mathbf{M}' \end{pmatrix} \tag{12.12}$$

and

$$\mathbf{h} = \begin{pmatrix} \mathbf{v}_f \\ \mathbf{M}'\mathbf{v}_\tau \end{pmatrix} \tag{12.13}$$

Then Eq. (12.11) becomes

$$U = k + \left(\mathbf{g}'_\beta + \mathbf{b}'\mathbf{S}'_\beta\right)\mathbf{I}_\beta \mathbf{H}\mathbf{I}_\beta \left(\mathbf{g}_\beta + \mathbf{S}_\beta\mathbf{b}\right) + \mathbf{h}'\mathbf{I}_\beta \left(\mathbf{g}_\beta + \mathbf{S}_\beta\mathbf{b}\right) \tag{12.14}$$

or

$$U = k + \mathbf{g}'_\beta \mathbf{I}_\beta \mathbf{H} \mathbf{I}_\beta \mathbf{g}_\beta + \mathbf{g}'_\beta \mathbf{I}_\beta \mathbf{H} \mathbf{I}_\beta \mathbf{S} \mathbf{b}_\beta + \mathbf{b}' \mathbf{S}'_\beta \mathbf{I}_\beta \mathbf{H} \mathbf{I}_\beta \mathbf{g}_\beta + \mathbf{b}' \mathbf{S}'_\beta \mathbf{I}_\beta \mathbf{H} \mathbf{I}_\beta \mathbf{S} \mathbf{b}_\beta$$
$$+ \mathbf{h}' \mathbf{I}_\beta \mathbf{g}_\beta + \mathbf{h}' \mathbf{I}_\beta \mathbf{S}_\beta \mathbf{b} \qquad (12.15)$$

The fundamentals and transients for actor and object can be treated as constants during the search for an optimal behavior to link the two. Then the derivative of Eq. (12.15) with respect to $\mathbf{b}$ is:

$$\frac{\delta U}{\delta \mathbf{b}'} = 2 \mathbf{S}'_\beta \mathbf{I}_\beta \mathbf{H} \mathbf{I}_\beta \mathbf{S}_\beta \mathbf{b} + 2 \mathbf{S}'_\beta \mathbf{I}_\beta \mathbf{H} \mathbf{I}_\beta \mathbf{g}_\beta + \mathbf{S}'_\beta \mathbf{I}_\beta \mathbf{h} \qquad (12.16)$$

Setting the expression equal to zero and solving for $\mathbf{b}$ gives

$$\mathbf{b} = - \left(\mathbf{S}'_\beta \mathbf{I}_\beta \mathbf{H} \mathbf{I}_\beta \mathbf{S}_\beta \right)^{-1} \left(\mathbf{S}'_\beta \mathbf{I}_\beta \mathbf{H} \mathbf{I}_\beta \mathbf{g}_\beta + \tfrac{1}{2} \mathbf{S}'_\beta \mathbf{I}_\beta \mathbf{h} \right) \qquad (12.17)$$

which defines the optimal behavior profile, given fundamentals and transients for actor and object.

Analyses by Heise (1985) have indicated that reasonable simulations of social interaction can be produced while treating $\mathbf{W}_{ff}$, $\mathbf{W}_{ft}$, and $\mathbf{W}_{\tau\tau}$ as identity matrices—the weights in the diagonals all being equal to 1.0—and $\mathbf{V}_f$ and $\mathbf{V}_\tau$ as vectors of zeros. For this case define

$$\mathbf{H}_1 = \begin{pmatrix} \mathbf{I} & -\mathbf{M}' \\ -\mathbf{M} & \mathbf{M}\mathbf{M}' \end{pmatrix} \qquad (12.18)$$

and $\mathbf{h}_0 = 0$. Then the solution for the optimal behavior profile is

$$\mathbf{b} = - \left(\mathbf{S}'_\beta \mathbf{I}_\beta \mathbf{H}_1 \mathbf{I}_\beta \mathbf{S}_\beta \right)^{-1} \left(\mathbf{S}'_\beta \mathbf{I}_\beta \mathbf{H}_1 \mathbf{I}_\beta \mathbf{g}_\beta \right) \qquad (12.19)$$

An alternative way of representing $\mathbf{H}_1$ provides a more convenient formulation for programming.

$$\mathbf{H}_1 = \begin{pmatrix} \mathbf{I} \\ -\mathbf{M} \end{pmatrix} \begin{pmatrix} \mathbf{I} & -\mathbf{M}' \end{pmatrix} \qquad (12.20)$$

whereupon the solution is

$$\mathbf{b} = - \left(\mathbf{S}'_\beta \mathbf{I}_\beta \begin{pmatrix} \mathbf{I} \\ -\mathbf{M} \end{pmatrix} \begin{pmatrix} \mathbf{I} & -\mathbf{M}' \end{pmatrix} \mathbf{I}_\beta \mathbf{S}_\beta \right)^{-1} \left(\mathbf{S}'_\beta \mathbf{I}_\beta \begin{pmatrix} \mathbf{I} \\ -\mathbf{M} \end{pmatrix} \begin{pmatrix} \mathbf{I} & -\mathbf{M}' \end{pmatrix} \mathbf{I}_\beta \mathbf{g}_\beta \right) \qquad (12.21)$$

12.1 Incorporating Settings

Smith-Lovin (1987c) showed that events change impressions of settings and that explicit consideration of the setting for an event changes impression-formation processes with regard to actors, behaviors, and objects. She also showed through *Interact* simulations that actions get adjusted appropriately when actors try to maintain sentiments about settings as well as about actors, behaviors, and objects of action. (See Smith, 2002, for a study of Japanese impression formation processes with settings.)

All of the previous derivations are the same when a setting is included in analyses, but matrices in Eq. (11.15) change composition, leading to changes in the compositions of other matrices. The left side of (11.15)—τ, defined in Eq. (11.9)—becomes a 12-element vector.

$$\tau' = \left(\hat{A}_e \quad \hat{A}_p \quad \hat{A}_a \quad \hat{B}_e \quad \hat{B}_p \quad \hat{B}_a \quad \hat{O}_e \quad \hat{O}_p \quad \hat{O}_a \quad \hat{S}_e \quad \hat{S}_p \quad \hat{S}_a \right) \quad (12.22)$$

Correspondingly, vector **f** defined in Eq. (11.8) also has twelve elements.

$$\mathbf{f}' = \left(\overline{A}_e \quad \overline{A}_p \quad \overline{A}_a \quad \overline{B}_e \quad \overline{B}_p \quad \overline{B}_a \quad \overline{O}_e \quad \overline{O}_p \quad \overline{O}_a \quad \overline{S}_e \quad \overline{S}_p \quad \overline{S}_a \right) \quad (12.23)$$

Additionally, vector **t** as given in Eq. (11.16) is expanded to include setting terms. Rather than show the expansion of Eq. (11.16), I use this opportunity to show the prediction terms used in *Interact* since 1991. These terms were inferred during least-squares equation estimation procedures, and they seem to provide more reliable simulations than terms inferred via maximum likelihood estimation procedures. For analyses without settings, the current version of **t** is:

$$
\begin{aligned}
\mathbf{t}' = (1 \quad & A_e \quad A_p \quad A_a \quad B_e \quad B_p \quad B_a \quad O_e \quad O_p \quad O_a \\
& A_e B_e \quad A_e B_p \quad A_e O_e \quad A_p B_e \quad A_p B_p \quad A_p B_a \\
& A_p O_e \quad A_p O_p \quad A_p O_a \quad A_a B_p \quad A_a B_a \quad \quad (12.24) \\
& B_e O_e \quad B_e O_p \quad B_p O_e \quad B_p O_p \quad B_p O_a \quad B_a O_p \\
& A_e B_e O_e \quad A_e B_p O_p \quad A_p B_p O_p \quad A_p B_p O_a)
\end{aligned}
$$

Equation (12.24) must be expanded as follows in order to conduct analyses that take account of settings.

$$
\begin{aligned}
\mathbf{t}' = (1 \quad & A_e \quad A_p \quad A_a \quad B_e \quad B_p \quad B_a \quad O_e \quad O_p \quad O_a \quad S_e \quad S_p \quad S_a \\
& A_e B_e \quad A_e B_p \quad A_e O_e \quad A_p B_e \quad A_p B_p \quad A_p B_a \\
& A_p O_e \quad A_p O_p \quad A_p O_a \quad A_a B_p \quad A_a B_a \quad \quad (12.25) \\
& B_e O_e \quad B_e O_p \quad B_p O_e \quad B_p O_p \quad B_p O_a \quad B_a O_p \\
& A_e B_e O_e \quad A_e B_p O_p \quad A_p B_p O_p \quad A_p B_p O_a)
\end{aligned}
$$

Additionally, coefficients in **M** are changed to the values that apply when settings are explicit.

Changes in the order and composition of other matrices in the derivations follow directly from these changes, and the revised derivations need not be presented in detail.

12.2 Self-Directed Action

Actions toward the self have been studied by Britt and Heise (1992), and by Smith and Francis (2005).

Self-directed actions have just two elements, actor and behavior (e.g., the doctor medicated himself), so the composition of **f** is as follows.

$$\mathbf{f}' = \begin{pmatrix} \bar{A}_e & \bar{A}_p & \bar{A}_a & \bar{B}_e & \bar{B}_p & \bar{B}_a \end{pmatrix} \tag{12.26}$$

and the composition of $\boldsymbol{\tau}$ is

$$\boldsymbol{\tau}' = \begin{pmatrix} \hat{A}_e & \hat{A}_p & \hat{A}_a & \hat{B}_e & \hat{B}_p & \hat{B}_a \end{pmatrix} \tag{12.27}$$

The vector of prediction terms currently in use is:

$$\begin{aligned} \mathbf{t}' = \big(1 & \quad A_e \quad A_p \quad A_a \quad B_e \quad B_p \quad B_a \\ & A_e B_e \quad A_e B_p \quad A_p B_e \quad A_p B_a \quad A_a B_e \big) \end{aligned} \tag{12.28}$$

Matrix **M** is 12×6, consisting of coefficients estimated from data on self-directed actions.

Again, changes in the order and composition of other matrices in the derivations follow directly from these changes, so the revised derivations are not presented in detail.

13

Optimal Identity

Instead of seeking an optimal behavior for a given actor and object, events can be constructed (or reconstructed) by seeking an optimal actor for a given behavior on a given object, or an optimal object for a given actor-behavior performance. Such identifications of people on the basis of incidents are called labelings by sociologists.

13.1 Re-identifying Actors

Consider first the problem of finding an optimal actor. Instead of drawing behavior terms from (f′ t′) as in Eq. (12.1), we must extract actor terms.

$$
\begin{aligned}
\mathbf{z}'_\alpha = \big(& \overline{A}_e \quad \overline{A}_p \quad \overline{A}_a \quad 1 \quad 1 \quad 1 \quad 1 \quad 1 \quad 1 \\
& 1 \quad A_e \quad A_p \quad A_a \quad 1 \quad 1 \quad 1 \quad 1 \quad 1 \quad 1 \\
& A_e \quad A_e \quad A_e \quad A_p \quad A_p \quad A_p \quad A_a \\
& 1 \quad 1 \quad 1 \quad 1 \quad 1 \quad 1 \quad 1 \quad A_e \quad A_e \quad A_p \quad A_p \quad A_a \big)
\end{aligned}
\tag{13.1}
$$

It is assumed that an identity is recalled from memory with transients equal to fundamentals, so Eq. (13.1) becomes:

$$\mathbf{z}'_\alpha = \begin{pmatrix} \bar{A}_e & \bar{A}_p & \bar{A}_a & 1 & 1 & 1 & 1 & 1 & 1 \\ 1 & \bar{A}_e & \bar{A}_p & \bar{A}_a & 1 & 1 & 1 & 1 & 1 & 1 \\ \bar{A}_e & \bar{A}_e & \bar{A}_e & \bar{A}_p & \bar{A}_p & \bar{A}_p & \bar{A}_a \\ 1 & 1 & 1 & 1 & 1 & 1 & 1 & \bar{A}_e & \bar{A}_e & \bar{A}_p & \bar{A}_p & \bar{A}_a \end{pmatrix}$$

(13.2)

The diagonal matrix, $\mathbf{I}_\alpha$, contains elements of $(\mathbf{f}'\ \mathbf{t}')$ that were not moved to $\mathbf{z}_\alpha$.

$$\text{Diagonal } \mathbf{I}_\alpha = \begin{pmatrix} 1 & 1 & 1 & \bar{B}_e & \bar{B}_p & \bar{B}_a & \bar{O}_e & \bar{O}_p & \bar{O}_a \\ 1 & 1 & 1 & 1 & B_e & B_p & B_a & O_e & O_p & O_a \\ B_e & B_p & B_a & B_e & B_p & O_a & B_a \\ B_eO_e & B_eO_p & B_pO_e & B_pO_p & B_pO_a & B_aO_e & B_aO_p \\ B_eO_e & B_pO_p & B_pO_p & B_pO_a & B_aO_a \end{pmatrix}$$

(13.3)

Assuming that behaviors reappear in interaction fairly infrequently, it is reasonable to treat the behavior transients as equal to fundamentals—that is, each behavior is recalled fresh from memory, as it is recognized. Then Eq. (13.3) becomes

$$\text{Diagonal } \mathbf{I}_\alpha = \begin{pmatrix} 1 & 1 & 1 & \bar{B}_e & \bar{B}_p & \bar{B}_a & \bar{O}_e & \bar{O}_p & \bar{O}_a \\ 1 & 1 & 1 & 1 & \bar{B}_e & \bar{B}_p & \bar{B}_a & O_e & O_p & O_a \\ \bar{B}_e & \bar{B}_p & \bar{B}_a & \bar{B}_e & \bar{B}_p & O_a & \bar{B}_a \\ \bar{B}_eO_e & \bar{B}_eO_p & \bar{B}_pO_e & \bar{B}_pO_p & \bar{B}_pO_a & \bar{B}_aO_e & \bar{B}_aO_p \\ \bar{B}_eO_e & \bar{B}_pO_p & \bar{B}_pO_p & \bar{B}_pO_a & \bar{B}_aO_a \end{pmatrix}$$

(13.4)

Equation (13.4) lets object transients differ from object fundamentals, and by this rendering of the re-identification problem an object person's circumstantial state as a result of past events affects the calculation of an appropriate actor. However, an alternative construction is that labeling processes ignore all events prior to the last event—the one that is being explained—in which case object transients also would be set equal to fundamentals.

$$\text{Diagonal } \mathbf{I}_a = \begin{pmatrix} 1 & 1 & 1 & \bar{B}_e & \bar{B}_p & \bar{B}_a & \bar{O}_e & \bar{O}_p & \bar{O}_a \end{pmatrix}$$

$$1 \quad 1 \quad 1 \quad 1 \quad \bar{B}_e \quad \bar{B}_p \quad \bar{B}_a \quad \bar{O}_e \quad \bar{O}_p \quad \bar{O}_a$$

$$\bar{B}_e \quad \bar{B}_p \quad \bar{B}_a \quad \bar{B}_e \quad \bar{B}_p \quad \bar{O}_a \quad \bar{B}_a \tag{13.5}$$

$$\bar{B}_e\bar{O}_e \quad \bar{B}_e\bar{O}_p \quad \bar{B}_p\bar{O}_e \quad \bar{B}_p\bar{O}_p \quad \bar{B}_p\bar{O}_a \quad \bar{B}_a\bar{O}_e \quad \bar{B}_a\bar{O}_p$$

$$\bar{B}_e\bar{O}_e \quad \bar{B}_p\bar{O}_p \quad \bar{B}_p\bar{O}_p \quad \bar{B}_p\bar{O}_a \quad \bar{B}_a\bar{O}_a \big)$$

In order to partition out an actor profile

$$\boldsymbol{\alpha}' = \begin{pmatrix} \bar{A}_e & \bar{A}_p & \bar{A}_a \end{pmatrix} \tag{13.6}$$

we define a selection matrix

$$\mathbf{S}'_\alpha = \begin{pmatrix} 1 & 0 & 0 & 0 & 0 & 0 & 0 & 0 & 0 & 0 & 1 & 0 & 0 \\ 0 & 1 & 0 & 0 & 0 & 0 & 0 & 0 & 0 & 0 & 0 & 1 & 0 \\ 0 & 0 & 1 & 0 & 0 & 0 & 0 & 0 & 0 & 0 & 0 & 0 & 1 \end{pmatrix}$$

$$\begin{matrix} 0 & 0 & 0 & 0 & 0 & 0 & 1 & 1 & 1 & 0 & 0 & 0 & 0 \\ 0 & 0 & 0 & 0 & 0 & 0 & 0 & 0 & 0 & 1 & 1 & 1 & 0 \\ 0 & 0 & 0 & 0 & 0 & 0 & 0 & 0 & 0 & 0 & 0 & 0 & 1 \end{matrix} \tag{13.7}$$

$$\begin{matrix} 0 & 0 & 0 & 0 & 0 & 0 & 0 & 1 & 1 & 0 & 0 & 0 & 0 \\ 0 & 0 & 0 & 0 & 0 & 0 & 0 & 0 & 0 & 1 & 1 & 0 \\ 0 & 0 & 0 & 0 & 0 & 0 & 0 & 0 & 0 & 0 & 0 & 1 \end{matrix}$$

and a vector registering non-actor terms in $(\mathbf{f}' \ \mathbf{t}')$

$$\mathbf{g}'_\alpha = \begin{pmatrix} 0 & 0 & 0 & 1 & 1 & 1 & 1 & 1 & 1 & 1 & 0 & 0 & 0 \end{pmatrix}$$

$$1 \quad 1 \quad 1 \quad 1 \quad 1 \quad 1 \quad 1 \quad 0 \quad 0 \quad 0 \quad 0 \quad 0 \quad 0 \quad 0 \tag{13.8}$$

$$1 \quad 1 \quad 1 \quad 1 \quad 1 \quad 1 \quad 1 \quad 1 \quad 0 \quad 0 \quad 0 \quad 0 \quad 0 \big)$$

whereupon

$$\mathbf{z}'_\alpha = \mathbf{g}'_\alpha + \mathbf{S}'_\alpha \boldsymbol{\alpha} \tag{13.9}$$

Substituting these quantities for the corresponding quantities in Eq. (12.17) or Eq. (12.19), we obtain the solution for the optimal actor. The parallel to Eq. (12.17) is

$$\alpha = -\left(S'_\alpha I_\alpha H I_\alpha S_\alpha\right)^{-1}\left(S'_\alpha I_\alpha H I_\alpha g_\alpha + \tfrac{1}{2} S'_\alpha I_\alpha h\right) \tag{13.10}$$

and the parallel to Eq. (12.19) is

$$\alpha = -\left(S'_\alpha I_\alpha H_1 I_\alpha S_\alpha\right)^{-1}\left(S'_\alpha I_\alpha H_1 I_\alpha g_\alpha\right) \tag{13.11}$$

13.2 Re-identifying Object Persons

The solution for an optimal object identity to fit a given behavior by a given actor is a straightforward variation of the solution for an optimal actor.

In particular, instead of z_α in Eq. (13.2), we use

$$
\begin{aligned}
z'_o = (&1 \quad 1 \quad 1 \quad 1 \quad 1 \quad 1 \quad \bar{O}_e \quad \bar{O}_p \quad \bar{O}_a \\
&1 \quad 1 \quad 1 \quad 1 \quad 1 \quad 1 \quad 1 \quad \bar{O}_e \quad \bar{O}_p \quad \bar{O}_a \\
&1 \quad 1 \quad 1 \quad 1 \quad 1 \quad \bar{O}_a \quad 1 \\
&\bar{O}_e \quad \bar{O}_p \quad \bar{O}_e \quad \bar{O}_p \quad \bar{O}_a \quad \bar{O}_e \quad \bar{O}_p \quad \bar{O}_e \quad \bar{O}_p \quad \bar{O}_p \quad \bar{O}_a \quad \bar{O}_a)
\end{aligned}
\tag{13.12}
$$

Instead of the diagonal matrix, I_α, in Eq. (13.5), we use

$$
\begin{aligned}
\text{Diagonal } I_o = (&\bar{A}_e \quad \bar{A}_p \quad \bar{A}_a \quad \bar{B}_e \quad \bar{B}_p \quad \bar{B}_a \quad 1 \quad 1 \quad 1 \\
&1 \quad \bar{A}_e \quad \bar{A}_p \quad \bar{A}_a \quad \bar{B}_e \quad \bar{B}_p \quad \bar{B}_a \quad 1 \quad 1 \quad 1 \\
&\bar{A}_e\bar{B}_e \quad \bar{A}_e\bar{B}_p \quad \bar{A}_e\bar{B}_a \quad \bar{A}_p\bar{B}_e \quad \bar{A}_p\bar{B}_p \quad \bar{A}_p \quad \bar{A}_a\bar{B}_a \\
&\bar{B}_e \quad \bar{B}_e \quad \bar{B}_p \quad \bar{B}_p \quad \bar{B}_p \quad \bar{B}_a \quad \bar{B}_a \\
&\bar{A}_e\bar{B}_e \quad \bar{A}_e\bar{B}_p \quad \bar{A}_p\bar{B}_p \quad \bar{A}_p\bar{B}_p \quad \bar{A}_a\bar{B}_a)
\end{aligned}
\tag{13.13}
$$

The selection matrix replacing S_α in Eq. (13.7) is

$$S'_o = \begin{pmatrix} 0 & 0 & 0 & 0 & 0 & 0 & 1 & 0 & 0 & 0 & 0 & 0 & 0 \\ 0 & 0 & 0 & 0 & 0 & 0 & 0 & 1 & 0 & 0 & 0 & 1 & 0 \\ 0 & 0 & 0 & 0 & 0 & 0 & 0 & 0 & 1 & 0 & 0 & 0 & 0 \end{pmatrix}$$

$$\begin{matrix} 0 & 0 & 0 & 1 & 0 & 0 & 0 & 0 & 0 & 0 & 0 & 0 & 0 \\ 0 & 0 & 0 & 0 & 1 & 0 & 0 & 0 & 0 & 0 & 0 & 0 & 0 \\ 0 & 0 & 0 & 0 & 0 & 1 & 0 & 0 & 0 & 0 & 0 & 1 & 0 \end{matrix} \qquad (13.14)$$

$$\begin{pmatrix} 1 & 0 & 1 & 0 & 0 & 1 & 0 & 1 & 0 & 0 & 0 & 0 \\ 0 & 1 & 0 & 1 & 0 & 0 & 1 & 0 & 1 & 1 & 0 & 0 \\ 0 & 0 & 0 & 0 & 1 & 0 & 0 & 0 & 0 & 0 & 1 & 1 \end{pmatrix}$$

The vector registering non-object terms in $(\mathbf{f}\ \mathbf{t}')$, corresponding to Eq. (13.8) is

$$\mathbf{g}'_o = \begin{pmatrix} 1 & 1 & 1 & 1 & 1 & 1 & 0 & 0 & 0 & 1 & 1 & 1 & 1 \end{pmatrix}$$

$$1 \quad 1 \quad 1 \quad 0 \quad 0 \quad 0 \quad 1 \quad 1 \quad 1 \quad 1 \quad 1 \quad 1 \quad 1 \qquad (13.15)$$

$$0 \quad 0 \quad 0 \quad 0 \quad 0 \quad 0 \quad 0 \quad 0 \quad 0 \quad 0 \quad 0 \quad 0 \quad 0)$$

Finally, the solution vector for an object is

$$\mathbf{o}' = \begin{pmatrix} \bar{O}_e & \bar{O}_p & \bar{O}_a \end{pmatrix} \qquad (13.16)$$

Now, corresponding to the solution in Eq. (13.10) we can construct the equation for an optimal object.

$$\mathbf{o} = -\left(\mathbf{S}'_o \mathbf{I}_o \mathbf{H} \mathbf{I}_o \mathbf{S}_o\right)^{-1} \left(\mathbf{S}'_o \mathbf{I}_o \mathbf{H} \mathbf{I}_o \mathbf{g}_o + \tfrac{1}{2} \mathbf{S}'_o \mathbf{I}_o \mathbf{h}\right) \qquad (13.17)$$

The parallel to the solution in Eq. (13.11) is

$$\mathbf{o} = -\left(\mathbf{S}'_o \mathbf{I}_o \mathbf{H}_I \mathbf{I}_o \mathbf{S}_o\right)^{-1} \left(\mathbf{S}'_o \mathbf{I}_o \mathbf{H}_I \mathbf{I}_o \mathbf{g}_o\right) \qquad (13.18)$$

14

Modifiers

14.1 Emotions

In affect control theory, emotion is a transitory affective and somatic condition that registers how an event makes one seem as compared to how one is supposed to be. A person's emotion combines with his or her situational identity, generating a transient impression equivalent to the transient impression created by the current event. Thereby the person viscerally experiences how the current event impacts on his or her identity. This conception can be represented schematically as follows.

$$\text{Emotion:} \quad \text{function}\left(\left\{\begin{array}{c}\text{Historically} \\ \text{Anchored} \\ \text{State}\end{array}\right\}, \left\{\begin{array}{c}\text{Event} \\ \text{Generated} \\ \text{State}\end{array}\right\}\right) \tag{14.1}$$

The historically-anchored state is the fundamental evaluation-potency-activity (EPA) profile

$$\mathbf{r}' = \begin{pmatrix} \bar{R}_e & \bar{R}_p & \bar{R}_a \end{pmatrix} \tag{14.2}$$

for the role identity that has been selected for the self in the situation. The event-generated state is the EPA profile

$$\boldsymbol{\rho}' = \begin{pmatrix} R_e & R_p & R_a \end{pmatrix} \tag{14.3}$$

for the transient impression of self produced by the event. The fundamental EPA profile of the emotion that is appropriate for the person after the event is

$$\varepsilon' = \begin{pmatrix} \bar{E}_e & \bar{E}_p & \bar{E}_a \end{pmatrix} \tag{14.4}$$

Then the schematic becomes

$$\varepsilon: \quad \text{function}(\mathbf{r}, \boldsymbol{\rho}) \tag{14.5}$$

This shows that emotion can be predicted from the fundamental profile for self and the transient profile for the post-event self.

The function that relates the three profiles is obtained empirically by predicting outcome transients, $\boldsymbol{\rho}$, for emotion-identity combinations (like angry father) from the profiles for the role identities, $\mathbf{r}$, (e.g., father) and the profiles for the emotions, ε, (e.g., angry). Such studies have been conducted in the U.S.A. (Averett and Heise 1987; Heise and Thomas 1989), Canada (MacKinnon 1985/1988/1998), and Japan (Smith, Matsuno, and Ike 2001).

The function consists of a linear combination of $\mathbf{r}$ and $\boldsymbol{\rho}$, plus interaction terms. Were there a single interaction term multiplying emotion evaluation times identity evaluation, the function could be represented as follows.

$$\boldsymbol{\rho} = \mathbf{d} + \mathbf{E}\varepsilon + \mathbf{R}\mathbf{r} + \bar{E}_e \mathbf{Q}_e \mathbf{r} \tag{14.6}$$

or, alternatively,

$$\boldsymbol{\rho} = \mathbf{d} + \mathbf{E}\varepsilon + \mathbf{R}\mathbf{r} + \bar{R}_e \mathbf{Q}_e \varepsilon \tag{14.7}$$

where $\mathbf{d}$ is a three-element vector of equation constants; $\mathbf{E}$ is a 3x3 matrix of coefficients for the emotion profile; $\mathbf{R}$ is a 3x3 matrix of coefficients for the self identity. $\mathbf{Q}_e$ is a 3x3 matrix of zeros except for row 1, column 1 which contains the coefficient for the interaction, $E_e R_e$. The interaction can be represented in either of the ways shown, as needs require.

More generally, nine interactions might be involved in the formation of a combination impression:

$$\bar{E}_e \bar{R}_e, \bar{E}_p \bar{R}_e, \bar{E}_a \bar{R}_e, \bar{E}_e \bar{R}_p, \bar{E}_p \bar{R}_p, \bar{E}_a \bar{R}_p, \bar{E}_e \bar{R}_a, \bar{E}_p \bar{R}_a, \bar{E}_a \bar{R}_a \tag{14.8}$$

These can be incorporated into Eq. (14.7) as follows. Construct a 3x3 diagonal matrix, $\mathbf{I}_{Re}$, that has the role evaluation $\bar{R}_e$ in each diagonal cell and zeros elsewhere; construct a similar matrix, $\mathbf{I}_{Rp}$, with $\bar{R}_p$ in the diagonal entries; and a third diagonal matrix, $\mathbf{I}_{Ra}$, with $\bar{R}_a$ in the diagonal entries. Construct a 3x3 matrix, $\mathbf{Q}_e$, that gives the coefficients for predicting E, P, and A outcomes from the interaction terms

$\bar{E}_e \bar{R}_e$, $\bar{E}_p \bar{R}_e$, and $\bar{E}_a \bar{R}_e$. Construct a matrix, $\mathbf{Q}_p$, that gives the coefficients for predicting E, P, and A outcomes from the interaction terms $\bar{E}_e \bar{R}_p$, $\bar{E}_p \bar{R}_p$, and $\bar{E}_a \bar{R}_p$. And construct a matrix, $\mathbf{Q}_a$, that gives the coefficients for predicting E, P, and A outcomes from the interaction terms $\bar{E}_e \bar{R}_a$, $\bar{E}_p \bar{R}_a$, and $\bar{E}_a \bar{R}_a$. Now the prediction equation can be represented as follows.

$$\boldsymbol{\rho} = \mathbf{d} + \mathbf{E}\boldsymbol{\varepsilon} + \mathbf{Rr} + \mathbf{I}_{Re}\mathbf{Q}_e\boldsymbol{\varepsilon} + \mathbf{I}_{Rp}\mathbf{Q}_p\boldsymbol{\varepsilon} + \mathbf{I}_{Ra}\mathbf{Q}_a\boldsymbol{\varepsilon} \tag{14.9}$$

or

$$\boldsymbol{\rho} = \mathbf{d} + \mathbf{E}\boldsymbol{\varepsilon} + \mathbf{Rr} + \left(\mathbf{I}_{Re}\mathbf{Q}_e + \mathbf{I}_{Rp}\mathbf{Q}_p + \mathbf{I}_{Ra}\mathbf{Q}_a\right)\boldsymbol{\varepsilon} \tag{14.10}$$

The alternative form comparable to equation Eq. (14.6) is

$$\boldsymbol{\rho} = \mathbf{d} + \mathbf{E}\boldsymbol{\varepsilon} + \mathbf{Rr} + \left(\mathbf{I}_{Ee}\hat{\mathbf{Q}}_e + \mathbf{I}_{Ep}\hat{\mathbf{Q}}_p + \mathbf{I}_{Ea}\hat{\mathbf{Q}}_a\right)\mathbf{r} \tag{14.11}$$

where the hatted Q matricies represent the same coefficients as in Eq. (14.10) in a different arrangement.

Solving Eq. (14.10) for $\boldsymbol{\varepsilon}$ defines emotion in terms of the fundamental self identity and the transient impression of self.

$$\mathbf{E}\boldsymbol{\varepsilon} + \left(\mathbf{I}_{Re}\mathbf{Q}_e + \mathbf{I}_{Rp}\mathbf{Q}_p + \mathbf{I}_{Ra}\mathbf{Q}_a\right)\boldsymbol{\varepsilon} = \boldsymbol{\rho} - \mathbf{Rr} - \mathbf{d} \tag{14.12}$$

or

$$\boldsymbol{\varepsilon} = \left(\mathbf{E} + \mathbf{I}_{Re}\mathbf{Q}_e + \mathbf{I}_{Rp}\mathbf{Q}_p + \mathbf{I}_{Ra}\mathbf{Q}_a\right)^{-1}\left(\boldsymbol{\rho} - \mathbf{Rr} - \mathbf{d}\right) \tag{14.13}$$

This shows that emotion is associated directly with $\boldsymbol{\rho}$, so emotions correspond to how events have affected the self—an interpretation that corresponds to intuitions (e.g., events that make one look bad also make one feel bad).

However, situational identities also influence emotions in several ways.

- People conduct themselves so as to keep transient impressions of themselves close to their identities, according to affect control theory. Therefore the fundamental self role profile, $\mathbf{r}$, can determine emotion by determining what transient impressions generally arise as an individual creates events in a situation.
- Additionally, the fundamental self profile influences the way that transient impressions of self translate into emotions. According to Eq. (14.13) the transient self is compared to the fundamental self, as reflected in the sub-expression $(\boldsymbol{\rho} - \mathbf{Rr})$. This suggests, for example, that people experience especially good or potent or lively emotions when events make them seem more good or potent or lively than their identity warrants.

- Equation (14.13) further shows that one's situational role identity influences the extent to which transient impressions of self translate into more extreme emotions, because the profile for the role is involved in the matrix inverse that acts as an overall multiplier in Eq. (14.13).

The impact of this last effect was examined by analyzing the simplified case shown in Eq. (14.7). The solution for emotion in this case is

$$\varepsilon = \left(\mathbf{E} + \overline{R}_e \mathbf{Q}_e\right)^{-1} \left(\rho - \mathbf{Rr} - \mathbf{d}\right) \tag{14.14}$$

Using empirical estimates of the coefficients in $\mathbf{E}$ and $\mathbf{Q}_e$ (from Heise and Thomas 1989), the determinant of the pre-multiplier is

$$\left|\mathbf{E} + \overline{R}_e \mathbf{Q}_e\right| = \begin{pmatrix} (.690 + .118\overline{R}_e) \times (.651 \times .530) \\ -(.69 + .118\overline{R}_e) \times (.069 \times .009) \\ -(-.181) \times (-.365) \times .530 \\ +(-.181) \times .069 \times .004 \\ +(-.042) \times (-.365) \times .009 \\ -(-.042) \times .651 \times .004 \end{pmatrix} = 0.041\overline{R}_e + 0.203 \tag{14.15}$$

When $\overline{R}_e = -4.951$ the determinant is zero, and the solution is undefined. This cannot happen since -4.951 is beyond the empirical range of identity evaluations (the measuring scale goes only to -4.3). However, as self evaluations get very negative the determinant gets close to zero, the values in the overall matrix multiplier become very large, and translations of transient self impressions to emotions are greatly magnified. The implication is that people who adopt extremely negative identities may experience chaotic emotions, or emotional lability.

This analysis indicates that emotional lability is a consequence of the $E_e R_e$ interaction. Since this interaction is less important for emotion-identity amalgamation in Japan than in the U.S.A., emotional lability may vary across cultures.

14.1.1 Characteristic Emotion

An individual would experience the characteristic emotion for an identity if the identity were perfectly confirmed. Perfect confirmation means that the identity transient equals the identity fundamental, $\rho = \mathbf{r}$. In such a case, Eq. (14.13) becomes

$$\varepsilon_C = \left(\mathbf{E} + \mathbf{I}_{Re}\mathbf{Q}_e + \mathbf{I}_{Rp}\mathbf{Q}_p + \mathbf{I}_{Ra}\mathbf{Q}_a\right)^{-1} \left(\mathbf{r} - \mathbf{Rr} - \mathbf{d}\right) \tag{14.16}$$

or

$$\varepsilon_C = \left(\mathbf{E} + \mathbf{I}_{Re}\mathbf{Q}_e + \mathbf{I}_{Rp}\mathbf{Q}_p + \mathbf{I}_{Ra}\mathbf{Q}_a\right)^{-1} \left((\mathbf{I} - \mathbf{R})\mathbf{r} - \mathbf{d}\right) \tag{14.17}$$

14.2 Attributes

Affect control theory treats a personal attribute—a trait, status characteristic, mood, or moral condition—as a trans-situational particulizer of identity. Comparable to the case given in Eq. (14.10), the EPA profile, $\mathbf{p}$, combines with the role identity that a person adopts, $\mathbf{r}$, and generates the fundamental profile, $\mathbf{f_r}$, that is to be confirmed in the situation.

$$\mathbf{f_r} = \mathbf{d} + \mathbf{Pp} + \mathbf{Rr} + \left(\mathbf{I_{Re}Q_e} + \mathbf{I_{Rp}Q_p} + \mathbf{I_{Ra}Q_a}\right)\mathbf{p} \tag{14.18}$$

The coefficients in the $\mathbf{P}$, $\mathbf{R}$, and $\mathbf{Q}$ matricies may have different values than they do in emotion processing.

In re-identification processes, $\mathbf{f_r}$ is interpreted as the EPA profile that accounts for a past event. This is the profile defined by Eq. (13.11) if re-identifying an actor ("Who would do such an action?") or by Eq. (13.18) if re-identifying an object ("Who befits such action?"). When those equations were presented, the profiles that they define were used to label the individual with a new identity. Now, however, the re-identification profile is viewed as an amalgamation of attribute and identity, and we seek to specify the attribute that combines with the individual's current identity so as to produce $\mathbf{f_r}$.

First we find the profile, $\mathbf{f_r}$, that is confirmed by a recent action, then we ask what attribute profile, $\mathbf{p}$, is required in order to convert the profile for the person's identity, $\mathbf{r}$, into $\mathbf{f_r}$. The solution is obtained via Eq. (14.10)—the same equation as was used in developing an emotion model, except we now change the symbols standing for emotion ($\mathbf{E}$, $\boldsymbol{\varepsilon}$, E_e, E_p, E_a) to symbols standing for other particularizers ($\mathbf{P}$, $\mathbf{p}$, P_e, P_p, P_a), and we change the $\boldsymbol{\rho}$ standing for a transient profile to $\mathbf{f_r}$ since we are accounting for an inferred fundamental state instead of accounting for a transient state. With these substitutions, and understanding the other terms as defined for Eq. (14.10), the solution is the same as for the emotion model, Eq. (14.13).

$$\mathbf{p} = \left(\mathbf{P} + \mathbf{I_{Re}Q_e} + \mathbf{I_{Rp}Q_p} + \mathbf{I_{Ra}Q_a}\right)^{-1}\left(\mathbf{f_r} - \mathbf{Rr} - \mathbf{d}\right) \tag{14.19}$$

The model has some implications regarding trait inference, as it did for emotions. First, the trait that is inferred in order to account for a particular event will vary depending on the person's initial situational identity. Thus, participating in the same happening in the same way could imply different traits for people with different identities. Second, trait inferences about a person with an extremely negative situational identity should be chaotic, depending on minor variations in participation.

15

Emotions and Re-identification

Re-identification, as considered in Chapter 13, makes no reference to emotional states that are observed while events confirm or disconfirm people's situational identities. Such a formulation is useful because in many instances emotional states are unknown, poorly appraised, or purposely discounted. In other cases, though, such a formulation is too simplistic.

> [W]hen we are present at the events that stimulate re-identifications or when we observe a person narrating his or her own behavior, we have access to the expressive signaling system that our species has evolved, and we obtain information about what emotions the person feels as a result of the events. ... Reassessment of the person's character must take account of the emotion displayed because the expressive behavior may cue us that the other feels disconfirmed by events rather than confirmed. (Heise 1989, p. 14)

This chapter incorporates information on observed emotionality into re-identification processes. When a target for re-identification maintains a particular mood while experiencing events, an observer tries to factor that mood into an inference about the identity that the target individual must have. For instance, a parent maintaining jubilance while disciplining her child may seem like a child abuser.

The problem parallels the attribution processes considered in Chapter 14. In the case of attribution, an action generates an ideal evaluation-potency-activity (EPA) profile for its actor, or object, and we solve for the attribute that yields the ideal profile, in amalgamation with the individual's identity. Here, the attribution is given—the observed mood—and we solve for the identity that amalgamates with the mood to produce the ideal profile.

A two-step approach was taken to attribution in Chapter 14: solve for the ideal profile, then solve for the attribute. Here a unitary and more flexible solution is provided. The EPA profile for the actor is defined in terms of the actor's mood, the EPA profile for the behavior performed, and the fundamental and transient EPA profiles for the object. Alternatively, the EPA profile for the object is defined in terms of the object's mood, the EPA profile for the behavior performed, and the fundamental and transient EPA profiles for the actor.

15.1 Inferences From Mood

Equation (14.11) provides the relevant formulation of the amalgamation of mood and identity for present purposes:

$$\mathbf{f}_{r\mu} = \mathbf{d} + \mathbf{E}\boldsymbol{\mu}_\varepsilon + \mathbf{R}\mathbf{r} + \left(\mathbf{I}_{\mu e}\hat{\mathbf{Q}}_e + \mathbf{I}_{\mu p}\hat{\mathbf{Q}}_p + \mathbf{I}_{\mu a}\hat{\mathbf{Q}}_a\right)\mathbf{r}$$

$$= \mathbf{d} + \mathbf{E}\boldsymbol{\mu}_\varepsilon + \left(\mathbf{R} + \mathbf{I}_{\mu e}\hat{\mathbf{Q}}_e + \mathbf{I}_{\mu p}\hat{\mathbf{Q}}_p + \mathbf{I}_{\mu a}\hat{\mathbf{Q}}_a\right)\mathbf{r}$$

(15.1)

Vector $\mathbf{f}_{r\mu}$ is the amalgamate EPA profile, $\boldsymbol{\mu}_\varepsilon$ is the EPA profile for the emotion defining the individual's mood, and $\mathbf{r}$ is the EPA profile for the individual's role identity. Vector $\mathbf{d}$ provides equation constants, and 3x3 matricies $\mathbf{E}$ and $\mathbf{R}$ consist of coefficients for weighting the first-order contributions of mood and role identity to the amalgamate. $\mathbf{I}_{\mu e}$ is a 3x3 diagonal matrix with the mood evaluation in the diagonal cells, $\mathbf{I}_{\mu p}$ is a 3x3 diagonal matrix with the mood potency in the diagonal cells, and $\mathbf{I}_{\mu a}$ is a 3x3 diagonal matrix with the mood activity in the diagonal cells. The $\mathbf{Q}$ matricies contain coefficients for weighting the second-order interactions of mood and identity EPAs in generating each of the three components of $\mathbf{f}_{r\mu}$; some or all of these coefficients may be zero. This framework, as contrasted with the one presented by Heise (1989), allows for all second-order interactions between mood and identity.

Since $\mathbf{f}_{r\mu}$ is a fundamental sentiment being maintained by the self in the situation, it can be substituted in Eq. (11.8) for the fundamental profile of the actor in an event.

$$\hat{\mathbf{f}}' = \begin{pmatrix} \mathbf{f}'_{r\mu} & \overline{B}_e & \overline{B}_p & \overline{B}_a & \overline{O}_e & \overline{O}_p & \overline{O}_a \end{pmatrix}$$

(15.2)

or

$$\hat{\mathbf{f}}' = \left(\left[\mathbf{d} + \mathbf{E}\boldsymbol{\mu}_\varepsilon + \left(\mathbf{R} + \mathbf{I}_{\mu e}\hat{\mathbf{Q}}_e + \mathbf{I}_{\mu p}\hat{\mathbf{Q}}_p + \mathbf{I}_{\mu a}\hat{\mathbf{Q}}_a\right)\mathbf{r}\right]' \right.$$

$$\left. \begin{matrix} \overline{B}_e & \overline{B}_p & \overline{B}_a & \overline{O}_e & \overline{O}_p & \overline{O}_a \end{matrix} \right)$$

(15.3)

The vector $\mathbf{r}$ is the fundamental EPA profile of the actor's identity

$$\mathbf{r} = \begin{pmatrix} \bar{A}_e \\ \bar{A}_p \\ \bar{A}_a \end{pmatrix} \tag{15.4}$$

so the amalgamate identity can be expressed as a function of the original $\mathbf{f}$ vector in Eq. (11.8) as follows:

$$\hat{\mathbf{f}} = \mathbf{\Phi} \begin{bmatrix} \begin{pmatrix} \bar{A}_e \\ \bar{A}_p \\ \bar{A}_a \end{pmatrix} \\ \begin{pmatrix} \bar{B}_e \\ \bar{B}_p \\ \bar{B}_a \end{pmatrix} \\ \begin{pmatrix} \bar{O}_e \\ \bar{O}_p \\ \bar{O}_a \end{pmatrix} \end{bmatrix} + \mathbf{\varphi} = \mathbf{\Phi}\mathbf{f} + \mathbf{\varphi} \tag{15.5}$$

given the following definitions:

$$\mathbf{\Phi} = \begin{pmatrix} \mathbf{R} + \mathbf{I}_{Ee}\hat{\mathbf{Q}}_e + \mathbf{I}_{Ep}\hat{\mathbf{Q}}_p + \mathbf{I}_{Ea}\hat{\mathbf{Q}}_a & \mathbf{0} & \mathbf{0} \\ \mathbf{0} & \mathbf{I} & \mathbf{0} \\ \mathbf{0} & \mathbf{0} & \mathbf{I} \end{pmatrix} \tag{15.6}$$

and

$$\mathbf{\varphi}' = \begin{bmatrix} (\mathbf{d} + \mathbf{E}\mathbf{e})' & 0 & 0 & 0 & 0 & 0 & 0 \end{bmatrix} \tag{15.7}$$

Equation (11.12), which interprets unlikelihood as a sum of deflections, can be rewritten using the amalgamated actor fundamental as follows:

$$U = k + \begin{pmatrix} \hat{\mathbf{f}}' & \mathbf{\tau}' \end{pmatrix} \begin{pmatrix} \mathbf{I} & -\mathbf{I} \\ -\mathbf{I} & \mathbf{I} \end{pmatrix} \begin{pmatrix} \hat{\mathbf{f}} \\ \mathbf{\tau} \end{pmatrix} \tag{15.8}$$

and substituting the expression from Eq. (15.5) gives

$$U = k + \left[(\Phi f + \varphi)' \quad \tau' \right] \begin{pmatrix} \mathbf{I} & -\mathbf{I} \\ -\mathbf{I} & \mathbf{I} \end{pmatrix} \begin{pmatrix} \Phi f + \varphi \\ \tau \end{pmatrix} \tag{15.9}$$

or

$$U = k + \left[\begin{pmatrix} \Phi f \\ \tau \end{pmatrix} + \begin{pmatrix} \varphi \\ 0 \end{pmatrix} \right]' \begin{pmatrix} \mathbf{I} & -\mathbf{I} \\ -\mathbf{I} & \mathbf{I} \end{pmatrix} \left[\begin{pmatrix} \Phi f \\ \tau \end{pmatrix} + \begin{pmatrix} \varphi \\ 0 \end{pmatrix} \right] \tag{15.10}$$

where 0 is a vector of zeros whose order matches the order of τ. Multiplying out gives

$$U = k + \begin{pmatrix} \Phi f \\ \tau \end{pmatrix}' \begin{pmatrix} \mathbf{I} & -\mathbf{I} \\ -\mathbf{I} & \mathbf{I} \end{pmatrix} \begin{pmatrix} \Phi f \\ \tau \end{pmatrix} + 2 \begin{pmatrix} \Phi f \\ \tau \end{pmatrix}' \begin{pmatrix} \mathbf{I} & -\mathbf{I} \\ -\mathbf{I} & \mathbf{I} \end{pmatrix} \begin{pmatrix} \varphi \\ 0 \end{pmatrix}$$
$$+ \begin{pmatrix} \varphi \\ 0 \end{pmatrix}' \begin{pmatrix} \mathbf{I} & -\mathbf{I} \\ -\mathbf{I} & \mathbf{I} \end{pmatrix} \begin{pmatrix} \varphi \\ 0 \end{pmatrix} \tag{15.11}$$

or

$$U = k + \begin{pmatrix} f \\ \tau \end{pmatrix}' \begin{pmatrix} \Phi' \Phi & -\Phi' \\ -\Phi & \mathbf{I} \end{pmatrix} \begin{pmatrix} f \\ \tau \end{pmatrix} + 2 \begin{pmatrix} f \\ \tau \end{pmatrix}' \begin{pmatrix} \Phi' & -\Phi' \\ -\mathbf{I} & \mathbf{I} \end{pmatrix} \begin{pmatrix} \varphi \\ 0 \end{pmatrix}$$
$$+ \begin{pmatrix} \varphi \\ 0 \end{pmatrix}' \begin{pmatrix} \mathbf{I} & -\mathbf{I} \\ -\mathbf{I} & \mathbf{I} \end{pmatrix} \begin{pmatrix} \varphi \\ 0 \end{pmatrix} \tag{15.12}$$

At this point we use Eq. (11.15) to express τ in terms of transients existing before the event:

$$U = k + \begin{pmatrix} f \\ \mathbf{M}'t \end{pmatrix}' \begin{pmatrix} \Phi' \Phi & -\Phi' \\ -\Phi & \mathbf{I} \end{pmatrix} \begin{pmatrix} f \\ \mathbf{M}'t \end{pmatrix} + 2 \begin{pmatrix} f \\ \mathbf{M}'t \end{pmatrix}' \begin{pmatrix} \Phi' & -\Phi' \\ -\mathbf{I} & \mathbf{I} \end{pmatrix} \begin{pmatrix} \varphi \\ 0 \end{pmatrix}$$
$$+ \begin{pmatrix} \varphi \\ 0 \end{pmatrix}' \begin{pmatrix} \mathbf{I} & -\mathbf{I} \\ -\mathbf{I} & \mathbf{I} \end{pmatrix} \begin{pmatrix} \varphi \\ 0 \end{pmatrix} \tag{15.13}$$

or

$$U = k + \begin{pmatrix} \mathbf{f} \\ \mathbf{t} \end{pmatrix}' \begin{pmatrix} \Phi'\Phi & -\Phi'M' \\ -M\Phi & MM' \end{pmatrix} \begin{pmatrix} \mathbf{f} \\ \mathbf{t} \end{pmatrix} + 2 \begin{pmatrix} \mathbf{f} \\ \mathbf{t} \end{pmatrix}' \begin{pmatrix} \Phi' & -\Phi' \\ -M & M \end{pmatrix} \begin{pmatrix} \phi \\ 0 \end{pmatrix}$$

$$+ \begin{pmatrix} \phi \\ 0 \end{pmatrix}' \begin{pmatrix} I & -I \\ -I & I \end{pmatrix} \begin{pmatrix} \phi \\ 0 \end{pmatrix}$$

(15.14)

This reduces to

$$U = k + \begin{pmatrix} \mathbf{f} \\ \mathbf{t} \end{pmatrix}' \begin{pmatrix} \Phi'\Phi & -\Phi'M' \\ -M\Phi & MM' \end{pmatrix} \begin{pmatrix} \mathbf{f} \\ \mathbf{t} \end{pmatrix} + 2 \begin{pmatrix} \mathbf{f} \\ \mathbf{t} \end{pmatrix}' \begin{pmatrix} \Phi'\phi \\ -M\phi \end{pmatrix} + \phi'\phi$$

(15.15)

Since the mood is treated as a given, ϕ is constant during the re-identification, and the last term may be absorbed into the equation constant. Doing this and rearranging terms gives

$$U = \hat{k} + \begin{pmatrix} \mathbf{f} \\ \mathbf{t} \end{pmatrix}' \begin{pmatrix} \Phi'\Phi & -\Phi'M' \\ -M\Phi & MM' \end{pmatrix} \begin{pmatrix} \mathbf{f} \\ \mathbf{t} \end{pmatrix} + 2 \begin{pmatrix} \phi'\Phi & -\phi'M' \end{pmatrix} \begin{pmatrix} \mathbf{f} \\ \mathbf{t} \end{pmatrix}$$

(15.16)

which has exactly the structure of Eq. (11.18), the generalized equation for unlikeliness.

Thus the solution for the optimal actor is given by Eq. (13.10) with **H** in Eq. (12.12) redefined as

$$\mathbf{H} = \begin{pmatrix} \Phi'\Phi & -\Phi'M' \\ -M\Phi & MM' \end{pmatrix}$$

(15.17)

and **h** in Eq. (12.13) as

$$\mathbf{h} = 2 \begin{pmatrix} \Phi'\phi \\ -M\phi \end{pmatrix}$$

(15.18)

15.2 Elaborations

The solution can be adapted to surmising the kind of identity an object person must have to maintain a given mood while being the object of action by another individual. In this case, the phi matricies adjust object-person fundamentals rather than actor fundamentals, and the H matricies are applied in Eq. (13.17) rather than in Eq. (13.10).

Heise (1989) pointed out an interesting property of the solution: the predicted evaluation of an actor is positive if the actor's mood is consistent with the impact of the actor's behavior (e.g., feeling ashamed during an act with bad consequences or joyous during an act with good consequences). The source of this effect is not obvious in the equations above, but I will return to the issue when presenting an illustrative analysis.

Analyses with the simulation program, *Interact*, have revealed another quirk of the solution: its solutions often are outside the range of actual identities. This, too, will be discussed later.

16

Self and Identities

During the definition of a situation, three factors influence an individual's adoption of a particular identity: the individual's efforts to actualize self, the space-time positioning of the individual within society's institutional structure, and alter-casting by influential others. This chapter formalizes the self-actualization process.

The basic proposition of affect control theory's self model is that individuals are motivated to enact identities with sentiments as close as possible to their self-sentiments. Enactments of identities that express the self-sentiment create a sense of self-actualization. Enactment of identities that fail to express the self-sentiment create a sense of inauthenticity for the individual. Accordingly, the motivational proposition can be restated as: Individuals select their identities in order to minimize inauthenticity.

In developing a model of identity selection processes, it is convenient to think of the evaluation-potency-activity space for identities as being re-centered at an individual's self-sentiment. Each identity profile, $\mathbf{r}$, is translated to identity profile ι in the individual's space by subtracting the profile of the individual's self-sentiment, $\mathbf{s}$.

$$
\begin{aligned}
\mathcal{I}_e &= R_e - S_e \\
\mathcal{I}_p &= R_p - S_p \\
\mathcal{I}_a &= R_a - S_a
\end{aligned}
\tag{16.1}
$$

In the individual's private space, the self is at the origin, and identities are vectors ranging outward, each directed toward relatively more, or relatively less, evaluation, potency, and activity than the individual's self sentiment. Each identity vector comprises a certain amount of inauthenticity, represented by its length, $\lVert \iota \rVert$.

An identity's potential for self-actualization is an inverted form of the identity's inauthenticity for the individual:

$$A_i = \frac{1}{1 + \|\iota\|} \tag{16.2}$$

where a value of 1.0 represents perfect self-actualization through the identity. A cut-off value, λ, less than 1.0—perhaps 0.5—can be viewed as the boundary of self-actualization.

16.1 Minimizing Inauthenticity

The recently-experienced-self is a vector, S, cumulating vectors for recently enacted identities:

$$S = \sum_{j=0}^{-n} w_j \iota_j \tag{16.3}$$

where sigma represents vector summation, n is the number of identities comprising the recently-experienced-self (a value greater than one), and w is a summation weight attached to each identity. Indexing for the summation starts at 0, representing the present, and goes backward in time, as represented by negative index numbers. Weights might be equal over the indexing range, or they might decline with larger negative indices to represent declining saliences of identity enactments further in the past.

Now the motivational proposition can be restated as follows.

An individual tries to minimize the inauthenticity of the experienced-self, i.e., $\|S\|$. This is accomplished by next enacting an identity as close as possible to $-S$.

If the individual can enact the ideal identity $\iota_1 = -S_0$ at time 1, then the inauthenticity at time 1 is

$$\|S_1\| = \|S_0 - S_0\| = 0 \tag{16.4}$$

The ideal identity, ι_1, would be a perfectly self-actualizing identity only if the experienced-self has zero inauthenticity at time 0. In general, an ideal identity absolves recent inauthenticities with its own inauthenticity in an opposite direction.

Since available identities rarely are ideal for an individual, the recently-experienced-self ordinarily is associated with some degree of inauthenticity. However, the recently-experienced-self can be considered self-actualizing whenever its magnitude is less than some value. From Eq. (16.2) and the definition of λ, S would be self-actualizing when

$$A_s = \frac{1}{1+\|S\|} > \lambda \qquad (16.5)$$

or

$$\|S\| < \tfrac{1}{\lambda} - 1 \qquad (16.6)$$

For example, if λ is 0.5, then the recently-experienced-self is self-actualizing as long as it is no further than one unit from the self-sentiment.

The weights, w, determine whether the system is stable or oscillatory. If the weights are all equal, then an enacted identity, ι, that drops out of the recently-experienced-self at time n+1 creates an inauthenticity $\|\iota\|$ that could be corrected by enacting ι again, and the system tends to be oscillatory. If weights decline for en-actments further in the past, then little inauthenticity is created when an enactment drops out of the recently-experienced-self, and the system tends to be stable.

17

Illustrative Analyses

17.1 Optimal Behavior

In this section, I show how the equations are applied by presenting a simplified version of the model dealing with evaluation alone. In this simple model the vector of fundamentals corresponding to Eq. (11.8) is merely

$$\mathbf{f}'_e = \begin{pmatrix} \overline{A}_e & \overline{B}_e & \overline{O}_e \end{pmatrix} \tag{17.1}$$

and the vector of post-event transients, $\boldsymbol{\tau}$, in Eq. (11.9) is

$$\boldsymbol{\tau}' = \begin{pmatrix} \hat{A}_e & \hat{B}_e & \hat{O}_e \end{pmatrix} \tag{17.1}$$

Impression-formation equations estimated only for the evaluation dimension, ignoring potency and activity effects and some interaction terms, are as follows.

$$\hat{A}_e = -.34 + .39A_e + .41B_e + .12B_eO_e$$

$$\hat{B}_e = -.27 + .12A_e + .55B_e + .11B_eO_e \tag{17.2}$$

$$\hat{O}_e = .11 + .61O_e + .05B_eO_e$$

Despite their simplicity, these equations explain a substantial portion of variance in post-event transients,—R^2 is 0.76 for actor evaluation, 0.81 for behavior evaluation, and 0.87 for object evaluation.

The **M** matrix in Eq. (11.15) is

$$\mathbf{M}'_e = \begin{pmatrix} -.34 & .39 & .41 & .00 & .12 \\ -.27 & .12 & .55 & .00 & .11 \\ .11 & .00 & .00 & .61 & .05 \end{pmatrix} \tag{17.3}$$

and the vector **t** in Eq. (11.16) is

$$\mathbf{t}'_e = \begin{pmatrix} 1 & A_e & B_e & O_e & B_e O_e \end{pmatrix} \tag{17.4}$$

The vector $\mathbf{z}_\beta$ in Eq. (12.2) is

$$\mathbf{z}'_{\beta e} = \begin{pmatrix} 1 & \overline{B}_e & 1 & 1 & 1 & \overline{B}_e & 1 & \overline{B}_e \end{pmatrix} \tag{17.5}$$

The diagonal of matrix $\mathbf{I}_\beta$ in Eq. (12.3) is

$$\text{diagonal } \mathbf{I}_{\beta e} = \begin{pmatrix} \overline{A}_e & 1 & \overline{O}_e & 1 & A_e & 1 & O_e & O_e \end{pmatrix} \tag{17.6}$$

The selection matrix $\mathbf{S}_\beta$ in Eq. (12.7) becomes

$$\mathbf{S}_{\beta e} = \begin{pmatrix} 0 & 1 & 0 & 0 & 0 & 1 & 0 & 1 \end{pmatrix} \tag{17.7}$$

while the $\mathbf{g}_\beta$ vector in Eq. (12.8) is

$$\mathbf{g}_{\beta e} = \begin{pmatrix} 1 & 0 & 1 & 1 & 1 & 0 & 1 & 0 \end{pmatrix} \tag{17.8}$$

Let $\mathbf{H}_I$ have the structure given in Eq. (12.18). Then its numerical value is the following.

$$\mathbf{H}_{Ie} = \begin{pmatrix} 1 & 0 & 0 & .34 & -.39 & -.41 & .00 & -.12 \\ 0 & 1 & 0 & .27 & -.12 & -.55 & .00 & -.11 \\ 0 & 0 & 1 & -.11 & .00 & .00 & -.61 & -.05 \\ .34 & .27 & -.11 & .20 & -.17 & -.29 & .07 & -.07 \\ -.39 & -.12 & .00 & -.17 & .17 & .23 & .00 & .06 \\ -.41 & -.55 & .00 & -.29 & .23 & .47 & .00 & .11 \\ .00 & .00 & -.61 & .07 & .00 & .00 & .37 & .03 \\ -.12 & -.11 & -.05 & -.07 & .06 & .11 & .03 & .03 \end{pmatrix} \tag{17.9}$$

Substituting these vectors and matricies into the solution for an optimal behavior defined by equation (12.19), and reducing, we get

$$\overline{B}_e = \frac{.02 + .41\overline{A}_e + .12\overline{A}_e O_e + .05\overline{O}_e O_e \atop -.11A_e + .07O_e - .06A_e O_e - .03O_e^2}{.37 + .03O_e^2}$$ (17.10)

Detailed examination of Eq. (17.10) indicates the following.

- The goodness or badness of predicted acts is dependent mainly on the actor's fundamental goodness or badness. Good actors engage in good behaviors, neutral actors engage in neutral or slightly good behaviors, and bad actors engage in bad behaviors.
- The actor's transient modulates these tendencies. Transient neutralization of a good actor exaggerates the goodness of the actor's actions when dealing with a positively evaluated object; this particular feature of the predictions was confirmed in a laboratory experiment (Wiggins and Heise 1987). Transient neutralization of a bad actor exaggerates the badness of behavior when dealing with a good object.
- Stigmatized object persons elicit behaviors that are evaluatively less extreme than behaviors toward valued object persons.
- Transient neutralization of an object relative to the object's fundamental causes behavior to be more extreme than it is when the object's transient and fundamental match.

17.2 Optimal Re-identifications

By a similar derivation, the solution corresponding to Eq. (13.11) for an optimal actor is

$$\overline{A}_e = \frac{-.17 + .12\overline{B}_e + .18B_e + .06B_e O_e}{.39}$$ (17.11)

Equation (17.11) indicates that object fundamentals are not a consideration in actor re-identification. For example, an actor who engaged in a given behavior on another theoretically would be judged the same, regardless if the other were a hero who has been made to seem neither good nor bad, or if the other were a villain who has been made to seem neither good nor bad. However, *Interact* simulations of actor re-identifications set transients equal to fundamentals for both behaviors and objects, as shown in Eq. (13.5).

When transients are set equal to fundamentals, Eq. (17.11) becomes

$$\overline{A}_e = -.44 + .15\overline{B}_e \left(5 + \overline{O}_e\right)$$ (17.12)

This reveals that object evaluations (ranging between ±4.3) never can reverse the judgment of an actor's character generated by the actor's behavior. However, the re-identification of an actor is more extreme with a good object and less extreme with a bad object.

The solution for an optimal object person as given in Eq. (13.18) reduces to

$$\bar{O}_e = \frac{.04 + .12\bar{A}_e B_e - .06 A_e B_e + .11\bar{B}_e B_e - .11 B_e^2 + .07 B_e}{.15 - .04 B_e + .03 B_e^2} \qquad (17.13)$$

Here again transients are distinguished from fundamentals. If transients are set equal to fundamentals, as is done in *Interact*, Eq. (17.13) becomes

$$\bar{O}_e = \frac{.04 + .12\bar{A}_e \bar{B}_e - .06\bar{A}_e \bar{B}_e + .11\bar{B}_e \bar{B}_e - .11 \bar{B}_e^2 + .07\bar{B}_e}{.15 - .04\bar{B}_e + .03\bar{B}_e^2}$$

$$= \frac{.04 + .06\bar{A}_e \bar{B}_e + .07\bar{B}_e}{.15 - .04\bar{B}_e + .03\bar{B}_e^2} \qquad (17.14)$$

Equation (17.14) indicates that for a nice behavior, re-identification of the object depends directly on the evaluation of the actor: good actors acting nicely suggest a positively evaluated object; evil actors acting nicely suggest a bad object person. For bad behaviors the opposite is true: a bad behavior by a good actor implies an evil object person, and a bad behavior by an evil actor implies a good object person. The denominator makes effects more extreme with moderately good behaviors.

17.3 Emotions And Re-Identification

I turn now to the matter of re-identification that accounts for emotion displays, applying Eqs. (13.10), (15.17), and (15.18) to just the evaluation dimension.

Equation (17.15) reproduces Eq. (15.1) for predicting the profile of an identity modified by a mood, except that Eq. (17.15) has a single interaction, of modifier evaluation and identity evaluation.

$$\mathbf{f}_{r\mu} = \mathbf{d} + \mathbf{E}\boldsymbol{\mu}_\varepsilon + \mathbf{R}\mathbf{r} + \mathbf{I}_{\mu e}\mathbf{Q}_e\mathbf{r} \qquad (17.15)$$

An empirically derived equation corresponding to Eq. (17.15), with no involvement of the potency and activity dimensions, is

$$\rho_e = -.50 + .42\bar{\mu}_e + .46\bar{R}_e + .11\bar{\mu}_e\bar{R}_e \qquad (17.16)$$

where $\bar{\mu}_e$ is the evaluation of the mood.

In Eq. (17.16), the arrays of Eq. (17.15) reduce to the following: vector d is (-0.50), matrix **E** is (0.42), matrix **R** is (0.46), and matrix $\mathbf{Q}_e$ is (0.11). Substituting the one-dimension estimates of **R** and $\mathbf{Q}_e$, Eq. (15.6) becomes

$$\Phi = \begin{pmatrix} (.46+.11\bar{\mu}_e) & 0 & 0 \\ 0 & 1 & 0 \\ 0 & 0 & 1 \end{pmatrix} \tag{17.17}$$

Substituting the one-dimension estimates of **d** and **E**, Eq. (15.7) becomes

$$\varphi' = \left[(-.50+.42\bar{\mu}_e) \quad 0 \quad 0 \right] \tag{17.18}$$

Combining these with the one-dimension **M** defined above in Eq. (17.3) allows **H** and **h** to be defined in terms of numbers and the variable, $\bar{\mu}_e$. The results are too unwieldy to display here.

Additional matricies are required to compute the solution for the optimal actor in Eq. (13.10).

$$\text{diagonal } \mathbf{I}_{ae} = \begin{pmatrix} 1 & \bar{B}_e & \bar{O}_e & 1 & 1 & \bar{B}_e & \bar{O}_e & \bar{B}_e O_e \end{pmatrix}$$

$$\mathbf{S}_{ae} = \begin{pmatrix} 1 & 0 & 0 & 0 & 1 & 0 & 0 & 0 \end{pmatrix} \tag{17.19}$$

$$\mathbf{g}_{ae} = \begin{pmatrix} 0 & 1 & 1 & 1 & 0 & 1 & 1 & 1 \end{pmatrix}$$

Now substituting quantities into Eq. (13.10) and reducing, we get the formula for predicting the evaluation of the re-identified actor when taking account of displayed mood.

$$\bar{A}_e = \frac{\begin{array}{c} .031+.120\bar{B}_e -.041B_e -.005B_e O_e -.024\bar{\mu}_e \\ -.023\bar{\mu}_e^2 +.045B_e\bar{\mu}_e +.013B_e O_e\bar{\mu}_e \end{array}}{.024+.015\bar{\mu}_e +.012\bar{\mu}_e^2} \tag{17.20}$$

or, assuming behaviors are processed with transients equal to fundamentals

$$\bar{A}_e = \frac{\begin{array}{c} .031+.079\bar{B}_e -.005\bar{B}_e O_e -.024\bar{\mu}_e \\ -.023\bar{\mu}_e^2 +.045B_e\bar{\mu}_e +.013\bar{B}_e O_e\bar{\mu}_e \end{array}}{.024+.015\bar{\mu}_e +.012\bar{\mu}_e^2} \tag{17.21}$$

The sign of the predicted $\bar{A}_e$ is more important than the actual value, since many of the predictions obtained with Eq. (17.21) are beyond the possible range of actual measurements: -4.3 to +4.3, even with inputs within the ±4.3 range. (However, the worst cases of blow-up involve mood-emotion evaluations between zero and -1, and most real mood-emotion evaluations are above or below this range.)

A pronounced consistency effect between mood and behavior occurs, when O_e is positive. An actor is re-identified positively when behaving agreeably while displaying pleasant emotionality, and an actor also is re-identified positively when behaving disagreeably while displaying unpleasant emotionality. On the other hand, an actor is re-identified negatively when behaving agreeably while displaying unpleasant emotionality, and an actor also is re-identified negatively when behaving disagreeably while displaying pleasant emotionality.

When O_e is negative, an actor is re-identified positively only when behaving agreeably and not displaying extremely unpleasant emotionality. An actor is re-identified negatively if behaving disagreeably or if displaying extremely unpleasant emotionality.

Thus this one-dimension analysis suggests that appropriate or inappropriate emotionality affects re-identification mainly if an actor is behaving toward a good person.

18

Programming the Model

A computer program, *Interact*, applies affect control theory's mathematical model to specific problems. The current version of the program consists of about 21,000 lines of Java code, mostly dealing with database management and the graphic user interface.

18.1 Organization of Analyses

An analyst begins *Interact* analyses of an interaction by choosing from lists of words the identities and the modifying characteristics of interactants and, optionally, the setting where the interaction occurs. Then the analyst identifies the actor and object in the initial event, with specification of a behavior being optional.

EPA profiles for the verbal inputs are retrieved from dictionaries to serve as sentiment measurements, and current impressions of actor and object are set equal to sentiments.

If a behavior was not specified for the initial action, an optimal behavior is obtained with Eq. (12.19), in order to complete the first action. Then impressions resulting from the action are computed with impression formation equations, as shown in Eq. (11.15), and the overall deflection produced by the event is computed with Eq. (11.18) with $k = 0$, identity matricies substituted for the $\mathbf{W}$ matricies, and zero matricies substituted for the $\mathbf{V}$ matricies. The impressions and the deflection are recorded in the simulation log.

Using Eq. (14.13), emotion profiles for an interactant are computed from the sentiment for the interactant along with the impression of the interactant that results from the current action. Emotion words with a similar profile are retrieved from the modifier dictionary, and these words are displayed. Additionally a face with an expression conveying the emotion is drawn on the screen.

The program predicts what interactants will do next by applying the equation for an optimal behavior—Eq. (12.19)—to the case of the current actor behaving again toward the current object, and to the reverse case of the current object behaving toward the current actor. Behaviors are reported whose profiles are close to the computed optimal profiles for each of these cases.

Re-identifications to explain the current action are obtained with the optimization equation for an unknown actor—Eq. (13.11)—and the optimization equation for an unknown object person—Eq. (13.18). Identities are reported whose profiles are close to the computed optimal profiles for each of these cases. Additionally, the re-identification profile for an interactant and the fundamental sentiment for the interactant's current identity are entered into the attribution equation—Eq. (14.19)—in order to define a modifier that explains the interactant's participation in the current action, and traits are reported whose profiles are close to the computed profile.

At that point, the analyst inputs a new action based on the displayed outputs, and the program computes the next round of interaction.

18.1.1 Emotionality Constraints

Analyses involving observed moods and emotions are conducted on a separate form in *Interact*. The form offers the following options:
- Find the optimal behavior when identities and specific emotions are specified for actor and object. This solution uses Eq. (12.19), after converting emotions to transients with Eq. (14.10).
- Find the optimal actor identity when the actor's mood is specified, the behavior is specified, and the object's identity and emotion are specified. This solution uses Eqs. (13.10), (15.17), and (15.18).
- Find the optimal object identity when the actor's identity and emotion are specified, the behavior is specified, and the object's mood is specified. This solution uses Eqs. (13.10), (15.17), and (15.18).
- Find the characteristic emotion for an identity. This solution uses Eq. (14.17).

18.2 Impression-Formation Equations

Impression formation equations are *Interact*'s means of determining how an action changes feelings about interactants, the behavior involved in the action, and the setting of the action. Equations also are available for predicting impressions created by combining an emotion, trait, or other personal attribute with an identity.
- ABO equations deal with actions specified in terms of actor, behavior, and object person;
- ABOS equations deal with actions specified in terms of actor, behavior, object person, and setting.
- AB equations deal with self-directed actions specified in terms of actor and behavior.
- MI equations predict the outcomes of combining a modifier with an individual's identity. In some cultures, different equations apply for emotions as opposed to personal attributes.

Program *Interact* reads impression formation equations in a tabular format that facilitates mathematical analysis. To illustrate, Table 18-1 shows *Interact*'s impression-formation equations for self-directed actions, based on data from U.S.A. males.

Each column of decimal numbers in Table 18-1 represents a different equation. For example, the first column of decimal numbers defines an equation for predicting how an actor will be evaluated after directing an action toward the self. The second column gives an equation for predicting how powerful the actor will seem after the self-directed action.

In the case of AB equations, there are six columns of decimal numbers, defining equations for predicting the evaluation-potency-activity (EPA) outcomes for the actor and the behavior. In the case of ABO equations, there are nine columns for predicting the EPA outcomes for the actor, behavior, and object person. In the case of ABOS equations, there are twelve columns defining how to predict the EPA outcomes for the actor, behavior, object person, and setting. MI equations have three columns defining the equations for predicting EPA impressions created by combining a modifier and identity.

Table 18-1. Tabular representation of equations for predicting evaluation, potency, and activity outcomes for the actor and behavior in a self-directed action.

			Post-Event Transient for			
Z-term	A_e	A_p	A_a	B_e	B_p	B_a
Z000000	-.31	-.57	-.19	-.45	-.53	-.26
Z100000	.47	.00	.00	.31	.07	.00
Z010000	.00	.37	-.07	.00	.22	-.06
Z001000	.00	.00	.57	.00	.00	.43
Z000100	.24	.16	.10	.29	.07	.07
Z000010	.00	.00	-.18	.00	.16	-.14
Z000001	.00	.21	.37	.00	.13	.45
Z100100	.08	.00	.00	.07	.00	.02
Z100010	-.06	.00	.00	-.08	.00	.00
Z010100	.00	.00	.02	.00	.00	.00
Z010001	-.07	.00	.00	.00	.00	.00

Each row in Table 18-1 corresponds to one predictor term in the equations, and the decimal numbers in that row are the coefficients for that variable in the different equations. Predictor terms may consist of a constant (the first row in Table 18-1), a single EPA variable (rows 2 through 7), or of products of EPA variables.

The column of zero-one numbers, preceded by "Z" identifies which EPA variables are in the term associated with a row, as follows.

- if the first digit has the value 1, then the term defined on that line involves the pre-event evaluation of the actor, A_e;
- if the second digit has the value 1, then the term involves the pre-event potency of the actor, A_p;
- if the third digit has the value 1, then the term involves the pre-event activity of the actor, A_a;

- if the fourth digit has the value 1, then the term involves the pre-event evaluation of the behavior, B_e;
- if the fifth digit has the value 1, then the term involves the pre-event potency of the behavior, B_p;
- if the sixth digit has the value 1, then the term involves the pre-event activity of the behavior, B_a;
- if the seventh digit has the value 1, then the term involves the pre-event evaluation of the object, O_e;
- if the eighth digit has the value 1, then the term involves the pre-event potency of the object, O_p;
- if the ninth digit has the value 1, then the term involves the pre-event activity of the object, O_a;
- if the tenth digit has the value 1, then the term involves the pre-event evaluation of the setting, S_e;
- if the eleventh digit has the value 1, then the term involves the pre-event potency of the setting, S_p;
- if the twelfth digit has the value 1, then the term involves the pre-event activity of the setting, S_a.

For modifier-identity equations, the rules are the same, with the substitution of "modifier" for "actor," and "identity" for "behavior" in the above rules.

To illustrate, the equation for predicting the outcome evaluation of an actor involved in a self-directed action is assembled from the materials in Table 18-1 as follows.

- The first column of decimal numbers contains the coefficients to be used in constructing the equation for predicting actor evaluation.
- The Z-expression on the first row consists entirely of zeros, indicating that coefficients in that row are equation constants. Thus the constant of the equation being constructed is -.31.
- The Z-expression on the second row has a one in the first digit followed by all zeros, indicating that the term represented in that row is the pre-event evaluation of the actor, A_e. Multiplying the term by its coefficient and adding to prior results, we get $-.31 + .47A_e$ so far.
- Coefficients in the next two rows are zero, so the corresponding terms can be ignored.
- In the fifth row, the Z-expression has a one in the fourth position only, indicating that the term for that row is the pre-event evaluation of the behavior, B_e. Multiplying this term by its coefficient and adding to prior results, we get $-.31 + .47A_e + .24B_e$ so far.
- Coefficients in the next two rows are zero, so the corresponding terms can be ignored.
- In the eighth row the Z-expression has ones in the first position and in the fourth position, indicating that the term for that row is the product of the pre-event actor evaluation and the pre-event behavior evaluation, A_eB_e. Multiplying this term by its coefficient and adding to prior results, we get $-.31 + .47A_e + .24 B_e + .08A_eB_e$ so far.

- In the ninth row the Z-expression has ones in the first position and in the fifth position, indicating that the term for that row is the product of the pre-event actor evaluation and the pre-event behavior potency, A_eB_p. Multiplying this term by its coefficient and adding to prior results, we get $-.31 + .47A_e + .24\ B_e + .08A_eB_e - .06A_eB_p$ so far.
- The tenth row is skipped because the coefficient is zero.
- In the eleventh row the Z-expression has ones in the second position and in the sixth position, indicating that the term for that row is the product of the pre-event actor potency and the pre-event behavior activity, A_pB_a. Multiplying this term by its coefficient and adding to prior results, we get $-.31 + .47A_e + .24\ B_e + .08A_eB_e - .06A_eB_p - .07A_pB_a$.

Thus the final equation for predicting the evaluation of the actor in a self-directed action is

$$\hat{A_e} = -.31 + .47A_e + .24\ B_e + .08A_eB_e - .06A_eB_p - .07A_pB_a \qquad (0.1)$$

The impression-formation equations used in *Interact* may be examined in tabular form by choosing View Equations from the *Interact* menu. The culture of interest should be selected first, since some culture-specific equations are employed in *Interact*.

18.3 Selection Matricies

Selection matricies, such as the one defined in Eq. (12.7), are constructed from the Z-expressions given in the tabular representations of impression-formation equations.

A zero-one matrix, **Z**, is formed at the beginning of an analysis as follows. The top part of **Z** (associated with fundamentals) consists of an identity matrix. The lower part of **Z** (associated with transients and their interactions) consists of Z-expressions used to define terms in the impression formation equations.

For example, when dealing with a self-directed action, **Z** consists of an identity matrix concatenated with the zero-one patterns displayed in column one of Table 18-1, as shown in Eq. (18.1).

$$
\mathbf{Z} = \begin{pmatrix}
1 & 0 & 0 & 0 & 0 & 0 \\
0 & 1 & 0 & 0 & 0 & 0 \\
0 & 0 & 1 & 0 & 0 & 0 \\
0 & 0 & 0 & 1 & 0 & 0 \\
0 & 0 & 0 & 0 & 1 & 0 \\
0 & 0 & 0 & 0 & 0 & 1 \\
0 & 0 & 0 & 0 & 0 & 0 \\
1 & 0 & 0 & 0 & 0 & 0 \\
0 & 1 & 0 & 0 & 0 & 0 \\
0 & 0 & 1 & 0 & 0 & 0 \\
0 & 0 & 0 & 1 & 0 & 0 \\
0 & 0 & 0 & 0 & 1 & 0 \\
0 & 0 & 0 & 0 & 0 & 1 \\
1 & 0 & 0 & 1 & 0 & 0 \\
1 & 0 & 0 & 0 & 1 & 0 \\
0 & 1 & 0 & 1 & 0 & 0 \\
0 & 1 & 0 & 0 & 0 & 1
\end{pmatrix} \qquad (18.1)
$$

Selection matricies are constructed by copying sub-matricies of $\mathbf{Z}$.

- The selection matrix for defining the optimal behavior, $\mathbf{S}_\beta$, consists of columns 4-6 of $\mathbf{Z}$;
- The selection matrix for defining the optimal actor, $\mathbf{S}_\alpha$, consists of columns 1-3 of $\mathbf{Z}$;
- The selection matrix for defining the optimal object, $\mathbf{S}_o$, consists of columns 7-9 of $\mathbf{Z}$. (This is not a defined operation in the case of self-directed actions.)

The $\mathbf{g}$ matrix that is required for obtaining solutions with Eqs. (12.19), (13.11), and (13.18) is obtained from the selection matrix, as indicated in Eq. (12.8).

The diagonal matricies $\mathbf{I}_\alpha$, $\mathbf{I}_\beta$, and $\mathbf{I}_o$ in Eqs. (13.5), (12.3), and (13.13) are obtained using the corresponding selection matrix in Boolean form. Java code for accomplishing this is given in Table 18-2.

18.4 Algorithms

Standard computational algorithms are used in *Interact* for matrix algebra. However, multiplications involving zero-one matrices are computed with the zero-one matrix in Boolean form, and computations are skipped when the value is zero. The final two lines of text in Table 18-2, above the closing brackets, show the method.

Table 18-2. Segment of Java Code From *Interact* for Computing Diagonals of Matricies $\mathbf{I}_\alpha$, $\mathbf{I}_\beta$, and $\mathbf{I}_o$

```java
// Fill I_diagonal with ones.
I_diagonal = new double[fullSize];
for (int i = 0; i < fullSize; i++ ) {
  I_diagonal[i] = 1;
}
// Loop through actor, behavior, object, and setting.
// Number of slots is 2 for AB event, 3 for ABO event, 4 for ABOS event.
for (int slot = 0; slot < numberOfSlots; slot ++ ) {
  // Loop through the EPA dimensions.
  for (int epa = 0; epa < 3; epa++ ) {
    col = (3 * slot) + epa;{
    // Skip over the unknown variables in the problem.
    if ((col < desiredSolution) | (col > (desiredSolution + 2))) {
      // Deal with the section of I_diagonal associated with fundamentals.
      I_diagonal[col] = thisEvent.abosFundamentals[slot][epa];
      // Now deal with the transient section of I_diagonal.
      // The range variable is number of fundamentals in the identity matrix of Z:
      // 6 for AB event, 9 for ABO event, 12 for ABOS event.
      // Start at range + 1 to allow for equation constant.
      for (int i = range + 1; i < fullSize; i++ ) {
        // Multiply selected transients.
        if (Zterm[i - range][col]) {
          I_diagonal[i] = I_diagonal[i] * thisEvent.abosTransientsOut[slot][epa];
        }
      }
    }
  }
}
```

Part 3

Researching Affect Control Theory

19

Growth of Affect Control Theory

Since the 1960s, more than 150 publications have reported research related to affect control theory. This chapter briefly reviews the research program, along with some related work on measuring affective meanings.

19.1 Chronology

Affect control theory is rooted in the work of psychologist Charles Osgood, who began studying bi-polar rating scales (or semantic differentials) in the early 1940s. Osgood was the senior author of a book, *The Measurement of Meaning* (Osgood, Suci, and Tannenbaum 1957), showing that ratings on such scales vary mainly along three dimensions—Evaluation, Potency, and Activity (EPA). That book initiated a burst of research in psychology that ultimately produced more than 1,000 books and articles (see Snider and Osgood 1969, for a bibliography). Later, Osgood was the senior author of a book, *Cross-Cultural Universals of Affective Meaning* (Osgood, May, and Miron 1975), which showed that the three dimensions underlie judgments of people around the world.

My own contributions began as a graduate student at the University of Chicago when I compiled a dictionary of affective meanings for 1,000 words, including scores of social identities and social behaviors. The sentiment measurements in that dictionary were instrumental in designing subsequent research studies. In 1967 at the University of Wisconsin I empirically defined equations to predict impressions created by events, extending work by psychologist Harry Gollob (1968). One of the papers reporting this work (Heise 1969a, p. 212) proposed that tensions produced by differences between impressions and sentiments summate psychologically, and "The basic proposition in tension theory is that persons strive to minimize tension." That was the first formulation of affect control theory, though the word "tension" has been replaced by "deflection."

In 1971 at the University of North Carolina I developed the mathematical model for minimizing deflection. The same year I gave my first public lecture on the theory at the University of Missouri—St. Louis. Herman Smith, now a prominent researcher on affect control theory, was a faculty member in the St. Louis audience. In 1972 I wrote a computer program to deploy the theory for simulation of social interactions—the first version of program *Interact*. In 1973 I privately distributed my report titled *Attitudinal Construction of Behavior Expectations: Working Papers*, consisting of 193 pages presenting the theory, the mathematical model including derivations for optimal actor identities as well as for optimal behaviors, and results of computer simulations.

In 1974 I assembled a new dictionary of more than 1,000 sentiment measurements for social identities and social behaviors. In 1975 I re-estimated the impression-formation equations with new data, allowing for multiple kinds of non-linearities.

In 1976 several graduate students affiliated with the research program, including J. Dennis Willigan (deceased) who compiled a dictionary of Irish affective meanings in 1977, and Lynn Smith-Lovin who began collecting data on impressions of settings. Smith-Lovin remains a prominent researcher in the research program.

An article in *Behavioral Science* was the first publication giving a detailed description of the theory. A John Simon Guggenheim fellowship in 1977 allowed me to begin preparing a book-length manuscript on the theory, and a grant from the National Institute of Mental Health supported a new round of data collection, with assistantships for graduate students who were engaging in various projects.

In 1978 Smith-Lovin derived complex impression-formation equations based on a new corpus of more than 500 event sentences. Variations of those equations still are in use today. Those working on the NIMH study collated sentiment measurements into a new dictionary of more than 2,000 entries, covering identities, behaviors, modifiers, and settings. In the same year Professor Neil MacKinnon of the University of Guelph, Canada, joined the research program while a Visiting Scholar at the University of North Carolina. He remains a prominent researcher in the program.

The first book on affect control theory appeared the following year— *Understanding Events: Affect and the Construction of Social Action* (Heise 1979). The book grounded the theory in the literatures of attitude research, symbolic interaction, and cybernetics; presented the mathematical model; and presented results of numerous computer simulations showing the theory's power for predicting behaviors in social interaction, and for predicting labeling of deviants.

Also in 1979 Smith-Lovin initiated her program of research on affect control theory at the University of South Carolina, focusing on developing databases, estimating variations of the impression-formation equations, and determining the effects of settings and sub-cultures. The first of Smith-Lovin's grants from the National Science Foundation supported some of this work.

In 1979 Steven Lerner began research with University of North Carolina political scientist Edward E. Azar and myself extending affect control theory to the domain of international relations. Lerner obtained successful results that were reported in his 1983 dissertation. Lerner's entry into the business world delayed publication of this work until recently (Heise and Lerner 2006).

In 1980 at Indiana University I extended the mathematical model to apply to settings, and to deal with trait attributions and emotions.

In 1981 MacKinnon initiated a large data collection project at the University of Guelph with funding from Canada's Social Sciences and Humanities Research Council. MacKinnon's work began coming to fruition in 1985 with compiled dictionaries of nearly 2,000 affective meanings, re-estimated impression-formation equations, and various studies related to affect control theory. MacKinnon's Canadian program of research on affect control theory continues today.

The second book-length publication on affect control theory, *Analyzing Social Interaction: Advances in Affect Control Theory*, edited by Smith-Lovin and myself, came out as a double special issue of the *Journal of Mathematical Sociology* in 1987. This publication contained articles by Smith-Lovin, MacKinnon, Christine Averett, Beverly Wiggins, and myself documenting the mathematical model, the newest impression-formation equations, expansions of the theory to settings, attributions, emotions, and likelihoods, and a laboratory experiment that tested and supported the theory. The publication was reprinted as a separate book in 1988.

Also in 1987 I created a program for measuring sentiments with computers, replacing less precise paper-and-pencil questionnaires. This data-gathering software eventually was used in Canadian, German, Japanese, and U.S.A. studies.

In 1988 Smith-Lovin and graduate student Dawn Robinson began experiments at Cornell University demonstrating the validity of affect control theory's prediction that individuals prefer to confirm their identities, even when that makes the actor feel bad. Robinson continues as a prominent researcher on affect control theory today.

Also in 1988 I extended the mathematical model for labeling deviants to take account of emotions and moods.

In 1989 Andreas Schneider compiled a dictionary of 1,000 German affective meanings at the University of Mannheim—data that were used for his doctorate at Indiana University. The database has been used to simulate German social interactions, with the aid of American impression-formation equations. Schneider remains an active researcher on affect control theory.

Herman Smith obtained the first of two Fulbright grants to visit Japan in 1989, where he began a research program on affect control in Japanese culture, in collaboration with Japanese sociologists Shuuichirou Ike, Takanori Matsuno, and Michio Umino. This group compiled a dictionary of nearly 2,000 Japanese affective meanings. Additionally, they empirically derived Japanese impression-formation equations for all components of affect control theory's mathematical model. Smith's work on affective dynamics in Japanese culture continues today.

As an Indiana University graduate student in 1992, Linda Francis applied affect control theory in her field work with California support groups for bereavement and divorce. She identified an affective structure for successful groups, independent of their ideology. Francis remains an active contributor to affect control theory.

In 1997 Amy Kroska completed her dissertation relating affect control processes to the division of labor in homes. Kroska continues to contribute to the affect control theory research program. The same year I re-wrote *Interact* in the Java programming language, incorporating facial displays of emotion into simulations, and made the program available on-line via the World Wide Web.

In 1996, with Smith-Lovin as a key instigator and planner, the General Social Survey included an "emotions module" consisting of 90 questions presented to a national probability sample of 1,460 respondents. Many reports of emotion analyses based on this survey have appeared, including an article by Kathryn Lively and myself. Lively, a post-doctoral fellow at Indiana University at the time of our study, continues as an active researcher in affect control theory.

In 1999, with funding from the National Science Foundation, Herman Smith began focusing on Chinese culture. Aided by Yi Cai in Shanghai, he compiled a dictionary of more than 1,000 affective meanings, using simplified Mandarin characters. Additionally he initiated a project to empirically define Chinese impression-formation equations—a project that continues today with the help of sociologists Luo Jar-Der and Wang Jin. In 2002 he and Luo Jar-Der began compiling a Taiwanese dictionary, employing traditional Mandarin.

In 2000, while a graduate student at the University of Arizona, Lisa Slattery Rashotte began her studies on how behavioral demeanor influences impression formation.

In 2001 I re-wrote the sentiment-measuring computer program in Java, giving it the capacity to obtain data over the Internet in world-wide languages. Thus far, this program has been used to collect data in Japan, China, and in multiple regions of the U.S.A. In 2006 graduate student Tobias Schröder at the Humboldt University of Berlin began using the program to collect a new German dictionary.

In 2002 Smith-Lovin and Allison Wisecup, a graduate student at Duke University, began inquiring into how multiple structural links between individuals might invoke simultaneous identities for each individual. Also, Smith-Lovin and Robinson began experiments on how individuals help manage the identities of others.

In 2003, Neil MacKinnon and I began examining how identities are organized within a culture, and how cultural organization of identities influences development of individuals' selves. We added a higher-order level to affect control theory's traditional model by proposing that an individual's self-sentiment, in conjunction with institutional settings, influences what identity is selected for self in a given situation.

Also in 2003, MacKinnon presented affect control theory as a framework for enhancing signs and other forms of knowledge presentation.

In 2004, Robinson began a program of research on tracking key variables in affect control theory in real time using physiological measurements. This research at the University of Georgia, with fellow faculty member Jody Clay-Warner, graduate students Christopher Moore, Tiffani Everett, and others, involves infrared thermography. Robinson, Clay-Warner, and Smith-Lovin also began a series of experiments looking at justice, over-reward and identity maintenance.

19.2 Branches

The following sections re-examine the affect control theory research program in terms of substantive areas.

Most of the research cited here was done with explicit reference to affect control theory. However, I also have included key publications regarding semantic differentials (see Snider and Osgood 1969, for a more complete bibliography), plus a few other especially relevant publications.

19.2.1 Measurement of Affective Dimensions

Several dictionaries of affective meanings are available on the Internet, via the *Interact* computer program (Heise 1997). *Interact* includes dictionaries for the U.S.A., Canada, Northern Ireland, Germany, Japan, and China. At the time I write this, no dictionary usable in *Interact* is available for a Spanish-speaking culture, none has been acquired from the Middle East or South Asia, and none from a nation in the former Soviet bloc, so research opportunities continue with regard to dictionary compilation. I have provided guidelines for assembling EPA data via the Internet (Heise, 2001; 2005) and with individual computers (Heise 1982b).

Printed compilations of affective measurements are provided by Jenkins, Russell, and Suci (1958), Heise (1965; 1978; 1979), Osgood, May, and Miron (1975), and Bradley and Lang (1999). Computer print-outs from Osgood, May, and Miron's (1975) study (sold at the University of Illinois Bookstore in 1975) give scales and EPA profiles for 610 concepts in Farsi, Turkish, Arabic (Lebanon), Serbo-Croat, Hebrew, German, Dutch, Spanish (Mexico City, Yucatan, Costa Rica), English (Illinois Whites and Blacks), Thai, Malay, Hindi, Bengali, and Portuguese.

The EPA dimensionality of affective responses is taken for granted in most ACT studies. Three publications by Charles Osgood and his colleagues mainly are responsible for this (Osgood, Suci, and Tannenbaum 1957; Osgood 1962; Osgood, May, and Miron 1975). However, the issue can be re-opened, and this was done by Wang Jin—now a professor at University, Wuhan, China—in his dissertation (Wang 2006) at the university of Iowa, under the direction of Professor Jae-On Kim and in collaboration with Professor Lee Myoung-Jin, Kookmin University, Seoul, Korea, and Professor Choi Setbyol, Ewha Womans University, Seoul, Korea. Other work relating to the validity of EPA space is worth noting. Chapman, McCrary, Chapman, and Martin (1980) examined neurological aspects of affective responses. Schneider (1999a; 2002b) examined the substantive meanings of different regions of the space.

The bibliography of *Semantic Differential Technique: A Sourcebook* (Snider and Osgood 1969) lists dozens of early publications on measuring evaluation, potency, and activity (also see Tzeng 1990). Reliability and other methodological aspects of EPA measurements have been discussed by DiVesta and Dick (1966), Heise (1966b; 1969b; 1970b), Smith, Ike, and Yeng (2002), Thomas and Heise (1995), and Walkey and Boshier (1969). A non-verbal system of EPA measurement was developed by Raynolds, Sakamoto, and Saxe (1981) and Raynolds, Sakamoto, and Raynolds (1988). Bradley and Lang (1999) used cartoon-anchored scales to measure the three dimensions.

19.2.2 Impression Formation

Impression-formation equations describe how affect is processed in individual's minds. Early work on impression-formation was done by Harry Gollob (1968; 1974; Gollob and Rossman 1973) and myself (1969a; 1970a).

Affect control theory does not assume that impression-formation processes are the same for everyone. While many similarities have been found across sex and across cultures, some interesting differences also have appeared in available studies (Averett and Heise 1987; Britt and Heise 1992; Heise and Smith-Lovin 1981; Heise and Thomas 1989; MacKinnon 1985/1988/1998; Smith, Matsuno, and Umino 1994; Smith, Matsuno, and Ike, 2001; Smith, 2002; Smith and Francis, 2005; Smith-Lovin 1979; 1987b; 1987c). Thus, new impression-formation studies are desirable in additional cultures and for samples of respondents of distinctive character. Smith-Lovin (1987b) provided a guide on how to conduct such studies. EPA data for such studies can be collected via the Internet (Heise, 2001; 2005).

Smith-Lovin and I (1982) developed a structural-equation model of impression formation. Heise and MacKinnon (1987) provided the sole study on predicting likelihood of events. Lisa Rashotte (2001; 2002a; 2002b; 2003) studied how demeanor influences impressions.

19.2.3 Theory and Mathematics

This book is the latest of my publications articulating the theory and mathematics of affect control theory (1977; 1979; 1985a; 1986; 1987; 1989; 1990; 1999; 2000a; 2000b; 2002). Others have engaged in this work, too, notably Lynn Smith-Lovin (1987a; 1990; 1991; 1993; 1994; 2002; 2003; Smith-Lovin and Heise 1988; Smith-Lovin and Robinson 2006), Dawn Robinson (2006; Robinson and Smith-Lovin, 1999; 2006; Robinson, Smith-Lovin, and Wisecup 2006), Neil MacKinnon (1994; MacKinnon and Heise 1993), and Clare Francis (2006).

Many of the publications referenced in other sections also make theoretical contributions (e.g., Rashotte, 2002a; L. Francis 1997). Some theoretical works outside the affect control theory tradition are ripe for integration (e.g., Demerath 1993).

19.2.4 Self

MacKinnon and Heise (2006) found that identities that individuals choose to characterize themselves are close to their self-sentiments in EPA space. Christopher Moore and Dawn Robinson (2006, p. 257) argued that "individuals seek out positions in society that they believe will provide them with the identities that match their existing self-views," and they found that inauthentic jobs are more distant from self-actualizing occupations than self-actualizing occupations are from one another.

The hypothesized interplay between inauthentic identities and redeeming identities is yet to be tested in a systematic empirical study. (A complementary hypothesis is that an individual's self-sentiment intermittently accommodates to changes in the experienced-self, in ways considered by Heise 2006.)

19.2.5 Computer Programming

Computer programs related to affect control theory have been documented in several places—both *Interact* (Heise 1978; 1982a; Heise and Lewis 1988; Schneider and Heise 1995) and programs for collecting EPA data (Heise 1982; 2001; 2005). Heise

(2004) and Troyer (2004) proposed affect control theory as a means of incorporating emotion into computer agents.

19.2.6 Experiments

Affect control theory has been tested via surveys, ethnographic research, and computer simulations, the citations for these studies appearing in other sections of this chapter. The theory also has been tested in several experiments (Robinson and Smith-Lovin 1992; 1999; Robinson, Smith-Lovin, and Tsoudis 1994; Wiggins and Heise 1987; Carter, Robinson, and Smith-Lovin 2006). I single out the experiments for special mention in order to encourage more work with this powerful method for establishing the validity (or invalidity) of the theory.

19.2.7 Emotions

Several studies have established that emotions have a three-dimensional structure corresponding to evaluation, potency, and activity (Osgood 1966; Morgan and Heise 1988; MacKinnon and Keating 1989). Lively and Heise (2004) replicated this structure with national survey data and demonstrated that the emotion space contains paths of emotional transition. Schneider (1996) employed the emotion structure in examining cross-cultural differences in sexuality.

Several essays present ACT's model of emotions (Heise and O'Brien 1993; Smith-Lovin 1990; 1993; Smith-Lovin and Robinson, 2006; Smith-Lovin, Robinson, and Wisecup, 2006). The model has been extended to mixed emotions (Smith-Lovin, 2002); to cross-cultural variations in emoting (Smith and Yap, 2006), to mental health treatment (L. Fancis 1997), and to empathic solidarity (Heise 1998). Lee and Shafer's (2002) study of greenway trail users found their emotions transitory, as predicted in affect control theory. MacKinnon and Goulbourne (2006) found that certain identities and relationships produce depression.

Normative emotions in particular situations and relationships have been the focus of a number of studies (Heise and Calhan 1995; Heise and Weir 1999; Lively and Powell 2006). The effects of inappropriate emotion on labeling was studied in everyday situations by Robinson and Smith-Lovin (1999), and also in a series of studies by Tsoudis, mentioned in the Deviance section below.

Rashotte (2001; 2002a; 2002b; 2003) examined the impact of emotional expressions and demeanor on impression-formation. Robinson, Rogalin, and Smith-Lovin (2004) examined the potential of physiological measures in studying emotions and other constructs in affect control theory.

19.2.8 Sub-Cultures, Gender, Ideology

Affect control theory accurately predicted behavior and emotions in two religious sub-cultures—Unitarians and gay fundamentalists—studied by Smith-Lovin and Douglass (1992). King (2001) linked features of Internet culture to sentiments associated with Internet identities and behaviors. EPA dimensions revealed underlying similarities in two different therapeutic ideologies (L. Francis 1997a; 1997b).

A number of studies have linked affect control theory to gender ideologies and sub-cultures (Kroska 1997; 2001; Langford and MacKinnon 2000; Smith, Umino, and Matsuno 1998; Smith-Lovin and Robinson 1992).

19.2.9 Life Course

Studies have dealt with the development of the EPA dimensions and with changes in sentiments during childhood (Di Vesta 1966a; 1966b; Maltz 1963). Heise (1985b) argued that adult displays of emotion socialize sentiments in children.

Heise (1987a; 1990b) viewed aging and institutional careers as processes influenced by sentiments about sequenced identities.

19.2.10 Social Structure, Social Change

Kemper and Collins (1990) linked evaluation and potency to the social structural dimensions of status and power. MacKinnon and Langford (1994) related EPA profiles for occupations to the occupations' prestige, education, and income. Liedka's (1995) multidimensional scaling analyses found EPA represented among several dimensions distinguishing occupations. Malone (2004) tied the EPA profiles of family identities to the gender, generation, and line of descent denoted by the identities.

Friedkin and Johnsen (2003) examined how influence networks can modify sentiments in a group. Robinson (1996) examined how sentiments attached to identities make some relationships more comfortable than others and thereby encourage the formation of affiliations and cliques.

Kirby and Gardner (1972) measured EPA profiles for ethnic stereotypes. MacKinnon and Bowlby (2000) analyzed how ethnic sentiments influence perception of group traits and the affectivity of inter-group interactions. Solley and Messick (1957) examined how the affective response to a classification of entities is affected by the statistical distribution of various features among the entities. Lovaglia, Youngreen, and Robinson (2005) proposed relations between performances in an identity and the sentiment attached to the identity.

MacKinnon and Luke (2002) examined changes in sentiments over a 15-year period in Canadian society.

19.2.11 Politics

Irwin (2003) and Troyer and Robinson (2006) provided general formulations of how affect control theory can contribute to political science. Schneider (1999c) applied the theory to the topic of neo-conservatism in the U.S.A.

Berbrier (1998) applied affect control theory in a study of White separatist rhetoric. Britt and Heise (2000) discussed how standard emotional transitions are used to advance social movements.

Lerner (Azar and Lerner 1981; Heise and Lerner 2006) demonstrated that affect control accounts for much of the variation in international cooperation and conflict. Heise (2006) extended Lerner's work to consider how relationships between nations can change.

19.2.12 Deviance

A series of studies (Tsoudis 2000a; 2000b; Robinson, Smith-Lovin, and Tsoudis 1994; Tsoudis and Smith-Lovin 1998; 2001) found that courtroom emotionality influences sentencing of offenders, as predicted by affect control theory's model of emotion-influenced labeling. Scher and Heise (1993) interpreted perception of injustice as an affective outcome, grounded in impressions of individuals' actions.

Gordon, Short, Cartwright, and Strodtbeck (1963) compared behavior sentiments of street-gang boys with middle-class boys (graduate student Heise served hot-dogs and sodas to the subjects in this study). Kalkhoff (2002) proposed new investigations of delinquent sub-cultures, based on affect control theory.

Marks (1965; 1966) measured psychopaths' self-sentiments and their sentiments about everyday concepts. Thomassen (2002) examined how participation in Alcoholics Anonymous influences sentiments about drinking. Schneider (1999b) found that Americans, more than Germans, affectively respond to sexuality in ways encouraging violence.

19.2.13 Language and Arts

Heise (1966c) examined EPA connotations of English phonemes. Lawson (1973; Lawson and Roeder 1986) measured EPA sentiments associated with men and women's first names and nicknames.

Heise (1966a) used sentiments associated with common words to analyze stories from the Thematic Apperception Test. Anderson and McMaster (1982) used the same data base to analyze the dynamics of stories and poems. Dunphy and MacKinnon (2002) considered ways to use *Interact* computer simulations in analyzing folktales and urban legends.

Elliott and Tannenbaum (1963) related the EPA dimensions to structural features of visual forms. Raynolds' projective differential (Raynolds, Sakamoto, and Saxe 1981; Raynolds, Sakamoto, and Raynolds 1988) revealed correspondences between various kinds of visual stimuli and sentiments.

MacKinnon (2003) outlined how affect control theory could serve professionals involved in knowledge presentation and signage.

19.2.14 Business

Smith (1995) examined how differing national sentiments can create stress in American-Japanese business relations. Schneider (2002a) proposed that differing national sentiments can create stress when local offices obey top-down edicts of multi-national corporations.

Clare Francis and Heise (2006) examined emotions produced by various kinds of work-place events.

20

Simulations

Researchers dealing with affect control theory often employ the theory's simulation program—*Interact* (Heise 1997)—to explore an issue and to derive hypotheses before they begin data collection. I used *Interact* to develop all of the examples that I created for this book.

Interact simulates social interaction, predicting what events might occur if people have particular identities, which emotions might arise during social interaction, and how people might re-identify each other as a consequence of events.

Interact removes complicated mathematical and database operations from an analyst's attention. The analyst describes people and events in words, and *Interact* makes predictions in words.

Yet everything that *Interact* predicts about social life is figured out quantitatively. Words given to the program are used to render the scene as a numerical problem. Then *Interact* employs equations that describe how feelings and sentiments combine and change, in order to derive predictions. Its predictions initially are in the form of numbers, but *Interact* translates numerical predictions into words.

Interact consists of a number of different screens, or forms, each devoted to a particular function. The next two sections of this chapter note the purposes of the various forms. (More details are available in *Interact*'s help system, available when using the program.) The final section of this chapter outlines factors involved in the credibility of *Interact*'s predictions.

20.1 Conducting Simulations

Five forms constitute the simulation system.

20.1.1 Define Interactants Form

Here the analyst sets the sex and appearance of each interactant. *Interact* can analyze social interaction among two, three, or four people.

If male sex is assigned to an interactant, then *Interact* uses evaluation-potency-activity (EPA) data obtained from males in order to represent how that interactant feels about things. Additionally, *Interact* uses impression-formation equations estimated from male data. If female sex is assigned, then *Interact* uses data from females to represent the person's sentiments, and computes the person's impressions with equations based on female data.

Choosing an appearance determines the face used to display emotional expressions. Several appearances are available for each sex. Facial expressions are formed from the EPA profile computed for an individual's emotion, according to the following rules: (a) open eyes with positive activity; (b) arch up brow with positive evaluation; (c) raise brow with negative potency, lower brow with positive potency; (d) move mouth higher with positive potency, and move upper lip higher with positive potency; (e) drop lower lip and narrow mouth with positive activity; (f) curve lips up with positive evaluation, down with negative evaluation.

20.1.2 Define Situation Form

This form lets an analyst specify how an interactant identifies self, others, and the physical setting. Identifications are specified by choosing from lists of identities, modifiers, and settings. Alternatively, numerical EPA profiles can be entered.

Specifying identifications for just one person yields simulation results that reflect that person's sex and definition of the situation. The situation has to be defined from the standpoints of multiple people in order to see how different gender sub-cultures interact, or to see how different definitions of a situation cause people to perform unexpected actions for one another.

20.1.3 Define Events Form

This form lets an analyst determine what events will occur, with three levels of specificity.

One option is to set no prior constraints on what two interactants will do, other than defining the actor and object of the first event. *Interact* offers its predictions regarding behaviors, and the analyst chooses the actor-behavior-object combination to occur next. *Interact* "implements" the chosen action, computing the consequent impressions, emotions, and deflections, and making predictions about behaviors in the subsequent event.

A second option is to specify the actor and object for each round of interaction, but to let *Interact* compute the optimal behaviors. The analyst chooses the specific behavior to occur in each round from a list.

A third option is to specify completely the actions that will take place. *Interact* then predicts impressions, emotions, and deflections resulting from those actions.

20.1.4 Analyze Events Form

The top of this form presents a list of events that have been defined. Clicking on an event has the following results.

- The emotions of the individuals involved in that action are displayed—as lists of emotion words, and also in the form of facial expressions.
- The optimal next action for the actor in the current event is presented in the form of a list of behaviors that best confirm sentiments, given impressions created by prior events, including the current event. Clicking on one of the behaviors creates a next event in which the actor performs the selected behavior on the current object. The new event is added to the list of events that can be clicked.
- The optimal next action for the object in the current event also is presented. Clicking on one of these behaviors adds a new event in which the current object is actor, performing the selected behavior on the current actor.
- Traits and conditions that help explain the actor's current behavior are presented as a list of modifiers. Clicking on one of the modifiers adds that attribute to the actor's identity.
- Traits and conditions that help explain the object person's current predicament also are presented, and clicking on a modifier adds the attribute to the object person's identity.
- A list of identities that could account for the actor's current behavior is presented. Clicking on one of the identities substitutes that identity for the actor's current identity.
- A list of identities that befit the object's current predicament is presented, and clicking one of these substitutes that identity for the object person's current identity.
- A graph shows deflections for all implemented events, including the current one.

20.1.5 View Report Form

This form presents a summary of analyses that have been conducted.

Each event is described verbally. Then the report shows the EPA profiles that were used to implement definitions of the situation, along with the transient EPA profiles and deflection that were produced by each event. The report gives EPA profiles for the emotions, expected behaviors, attributions, and labels arising from each event, along with a word corresponding to each computed profile.

20.2 Other Capabilities

Interact offers some capabilities that complement its simulations of social interaction, as well as some auxiliary functions.

- Import / Export Form. This form allows an analyst to import dictionaries of EPA profiles for use in simulations. An imported dictionary may supplement or replace one of *Interact*'s built-in dictionaries. This form also allows a user to obtain electronic copies of the built-in dictionaries. At the time of this writing, *Interact*'s built-in dictionaries consisted of two U.S.A. dictionaries from different eras, two Canadian dictionaries from different eras, plus dictionaries from Northern Ireland, Germany, Japan, and China.

- View Equations Form. The impression formation equations that are used in simulations can be viewed with this form. This form also can be used to input different equations.
- Select Options Form. This form can be used to set options that are useful when running large numbers of simulations. Also an option can be selected that has *Interact* learn new sentiments from events occurring during a simulation.
- Find Concepts Form. Entering an EPA profile on this form results in *Interact* creating a list of dictionary entries with similar EPA profiles. Retrievals can be restricted to identities, settings, or behaviors, and filtered by relevance to different social institutions. Alternatively modifiers can be retrieved, filtered according to whether they are emotions, traits, or status characteristics.
- Mood-Emotions Form. This form investigates how moods and emotions influence behavior expectations and re-identifications. *Interact* will find the ideal behavior for a given actor and object, when they are experiencing specified emotions. Alternatively, *Interact* will compute the ideal identity for an actor who engages in a given behavior on a given object, with the actor in a specified mood and the object person experiencing a specified emotion. (The same kind of solution can be obtained for the object person.) This form also can be used to find the characteristic emotion for an identity.
- Explore a Self Form. This form presents a circular graphic. A blue dot in the center represents an individual's self sentiment. The self sentiment can be changed by entering a new EPA profile in a field at the bottom of the form. A small green circle encloses identities that are self-actualizing for an individual with that self sentiment. A large yellow circle encompasses identities that might be within the individual's identity rounds. Clicking an identity highlights it in red. Simultaneously, identities on the other side of the circle are highlighted in black if they are identities that could compensate for inauthentic experience with the identity in red.

20.3 Errors

Interact results sometimes are implausible, for any of the following reasons.
- Theoretical errors. The principle that people try to confirm their sentiments has received considerable empirical support, but some specific aspect of affect control theory still may be wrong.
- Cultural variations in ratings. *Interact*'s predictions derive from culturally-based EPA profiles for identities, behaviors, modifiers, and settings. If the sentiments represented in these profiles are different than your own, then simulation results will seem wrong to you because *Interact* is describing a culture that is foreign to you.
- Errors in ratings. A culture's EPA profiles are estimated as averaged ratings from samples of individuals. By a fluke of chance all raters could have had the same

bias for some concept involved in a simulation, thereby causing a prediction error.

- Errors in equations. *Interact* incorporates human psychology through impression-formation equations that describe how feelings about things change as a result of events. These equations are defined through empirical research, which is subject to various kinds of problems that could produce errors in the equations, causing predictions to be erroneous.

- Lexical errors. *Interact* makes concrete verbal predictions, and some errors arise because the program cannot incorporate every rule governing word usage. For example, you could come upon an *Interact* prediction that one person "buries" another which is bizarre because "bury" should not be used as a verb describing social interaction. *Interact* screens words in terms of the kinds of the social institutions that are operative, eliminating the worst errors of this kind. However, misusages still creep in and make some *Interact* predictions look strange.

- Your own misconceptions. For example, *Interact* predicts that others may assign a stigmatized identity to the victim of a deviant act. You might believe that this is an error because it is unjust—the victim should not be blamed. But in this case YOU would be wrong. *Interact* correctly predicts derogation of the victim, a phenomenon that actually occurs among humans.

20.3.1 Versions of *Interact*

Publications on affect control theory present simulation results obtained with numerous different versions of *Interact*. If you repeat a simulation using the latest version of *Interact*, you will get results that are similar, but not identical to those obtained with earlier versions of *Interact*. Why doesn't every version of *Interact* give the same results?

- Equations might be different. For example, early versions of *Interact* used equations derived with maximum likelihood estimation, whereas later versions employ equations derived with more stable least-squares estimations.

- Sentiment measures might be different. For example, dictionaries of U.S.A. sentiments obtained in the 1970s can produce different results than a U.S.A. dictionary obtained in the 21st century because some American sentiments have changed over time.

- Cognitive filters for reducing inappropriate predictions might be different. For example, early versions of *Interact* coded relationships as verbal, physical, primary, exchange, managing, fixing, or training, whereas more recent versions use a system based on social institutions: Lay, Business, Law, Politics, Academe, Medicine, Religion, Family, and Sexuality.

- The program's design might have changed. For example, *Interact* reports words whose EPA profiles are closest to an ideal profile, stopping at an arbitrary criterion, and the criterion has changed in different versions of *Interact*.

- A programming bug might have affected results in one version. Eliminating bugs in software continues even after a program is made available publicly, and debugging re-starts every time the program is re-constructed in a new computer language. During its three decades of existence, *Interact* has been programmed in five different computer languages in order to keep abreast of computer developments.

20.4 Further Readings

Andreas Schneider and Heise (2002) published a detailed description of *Interact*'s design. Additionally Heise (2004) published a description of how *Interact* generates emotional expressions on faces. The program itself is available for use on the World Wide Web (Heise 1997).

Appendix

Basic Concepts in Affect Control Theory

Following are some central concepts in affect control theory, with brief characterizations of their usage in the theory.

Action: A human actor performing a behavior toward some object, possibly with explicit recognition of the setting in which the behavior occurs.

Activity: See EPA dimensions.

Affect: Emotions, sentiments, impressions, and motives.

Affective meaning: The connotation of a word or symbol, measured as an evaluation-potency-activity (EPA) profile.

Amalgamate: To combine several affective meanings in order to produce a new affective meaning. For example, a modifier paired with a noun, as in "loyal employee," yields a new affective meaning.

Attributes: Personality traits, moods, status characteristics, and moral dispositions.

Behavior: Focused activity by an actor toward an object.

Inconsistency: Two elements in an action having opposite connotations on the evaluation, potency, or activity dimension of affective meaning. For example, helping a murderer is evaluatively inconsistent.

Control: Resisting changes from the environment or attaining a goal state. Affect control theory focuses on resisting changes in affective meanings and actualizing sentiments.

Culture: The totality of socially transmitted meanings regarding people, processes, and non-human objects. Affect control theory focuses on affective meanings but also gives consideration to denotative meanings.

Deflection: Divergence of transient affective meaning from fundamental affective meaning. Informally, deflection may refer to a discrepancy on a single evaluation-potency-activity (EPA) dimension, or to the sum of an entity's discrepancies on all three EPA dimensions, or to discrepancies on EPA dimensions summed over all entities in an action. Formally, only the last interpretation is correct.

Denotative meaning: Rules for applying a concept to an entity. The rules may include logical implications and prototypical actions linking the entity to other entities.

Dictionary: In affect control theory, a database of words and their affective meanings measured as evaluation-potency-activity profiles, along with classifications of nouns and verbs into social institutions (e.g., religion, academia).

Distance: The difference between two evaluation-potency-activity (EPA) profiles. Distance is quantified as the square root of the sum of squared differences on each of the EPA dimensions.

Emotion: A temporary condition of an individual involving a somatic state, including a facial expression, and a transient affective meaning of the self.

EPA dimensions: Evaluation, Potency, and Activity measures. Evaluation ranges from infinitely good to infinitely bad; Potency ranges from infinitely powerful to infinitely powerless; and Activity ranges from infinitely active to infinitely passive. These three dimensions of affective meaning are universal across cultures.

EPA profile: A set of three numbers quantitatively defining an entity's affective meaning. The first number is an Evaluation measurement, the second is Potency, the third Activity.

Evaluation: See EPA dimensions.

Event: A human or non-human agent processing some object.

Feeling: Synonymous with transient affective meaning in affect control theory.

Fundamental affective meaning: The persistent affective meaning of an entity that serves as a reference for assessing a transient affective meaning. May be called a sentiment.

Identities: Culturally-defined categories of people.

Impression: Synonymous with transient affective meaning in affect control theory.

Impression formation: New affective meanings of actor, behavior, object, and setting emerging from an action.

Impression-formation equation: An equation that predicts the outcome evaluation, potency, or activity of an event element from pre-event evaluation, potency, and activity measurements of event elements.

Institution: An element of a society's social structure consisting of inter-related social settings, identities, and behaviors.

Interact: A computer program that implements affect control theory for the purpose of analyzing social interaction.

Likelihood: In affect control theory, the subjective probability of an action.

Macroaction: An action in which the behavior of an actor toward an object is implemented by a third party. The third party can range from an individual to a complex social organization in an ongoing establishment.

Mood: A fundamental affective meaning of the self obtained by amalgamating an emotion with one's situational identity. Moods persist longer than emotions, but not as long as one's sentiment about an identity or about the self.

Optimal solution: A behavior or identity that maximally confirms sentiments.

Potency: See EPA dimensions.

Re-identification: Replacement of an individual's fundamental affective meaning to better account for recent actions. This may be accomplished by assigning a new identity to the individual, or by amalgamating a modifier with the individual's current identity, where the modifier specifies a trait, mood, status characteristic, or moral condition.

Role : The set of actions expected of someone with a given identity in a given institutional setting. In affect control theory a role consists of institutionally appropriate actions that optimally maintain an identity's fundamental affective meaning.

Self: The complex of mental processes and actions orienting around the personal identity signified by an individual's name.

Self-directed action: A behavior directed at oneself rather than an external person.

Self-sentiment: The sentiment associated with an individual's personal identity.

Sentiment: Synonymous with fundamental affective meaning.

Settings: Culturally-defined categories of place or time.

Simulations: In affect control theory, analyses of social interaction obtained with the *Interact* computer program.

Situation: The interpretations of setting and interactants' identities that control an individual's actions in a social encounter. Defining the situation is a prerequisite for meaningful social interaction.

Stress: Unresolvable disruption of affective meanings; persistent deflection.

Sub-culture: Distinctive meanings within a group regarding people, processes, and non-human objects that have special significance within the group.

Trait: A personality type attributed to someone in order to adjust the fundamental affective meanings of that individual across situations.

Transient affective meaning: A momentary affective meaning resulting from action, generated by processes of impression-formation.

References

Anderson, C. W. and McMaster, G. E. (1982) Computer assisted modeling of affective tone in written documents. Computers and the Humanities 16, 1-9.

Averett, C. P. and Heise, D. R. (1987) Modified social identities: Amalgamations, attributions, and emotions. Journal of Mathematical Sociology 13, 103-132.

Azar, E. E. and Lerner, S. J. (1981) The Use of Semantic Dimensions in the Scaling of International Events. International Interactions 7, 361-378.

Bales, R. F. (1999) *Social Interaction Systems: Theory and Measurement.* Transaction, New York.

Berbrier, M. (1998) 'Half the battle': Cultural resonance, framing processes, and ethnic affectations in contemporary white separatist rhetoric. Social Problems 45, 431-450.

Bradley, M. M. and Lang, P. J. (1999) Affective norms for English words (ANEW): Stimuli, instruction manual and affective ratings. Center for Research in Psychophysiology, University of Florida, Gainesville, FL.

Britt, L. and Heise, D. R. (1992) Impressions of self-directed action. Social Psychology Quarterly 55, 335-350.

Britt, L. and Heise, D. R. (2000) From shame to pride in identity politics. In: S. Stryker, T. J. Owens and R. W. White (Eds.), *Self, Identity, and Social Movements.* University of Minnesota Press, Minneapolis, pp. 252-268.

Carter, W. C., Robinson, D. T. and Smith-Lovin, L. (2006) Restoring the challenged identity of others: Predicting restorative behaviors. Department of Sociology, University of Georgia, Athens, GA.

Chapman, R. M., McCrary, J. W., Chapman, J. A. and Martin, J. K. (1980) Behavioral and neural analyses of connotative meaning: Word classes and rating scales. Brain and Language 11, 319-339.

Demerath, L. (1993) Knowledge-based affect: Cognitive origins of 'Good' and 'Bad'. Social Psychology Quarterly 56, 136-147.

Demo, D. H. (1992) The self-concept over time: Research issues and directions. Annual Review of Sociology 18, 303-26.

Di Vesta, F. J. (1966a) A developmental study of the semantic structure of children. Journal of Verbal Learning and Verbal Behavior 5, 249-259.

Di Vesta, F. J. (1966b) A normative study of 220 concepts rated on the semantic differential by children in grades 2 through 7. Journal of Genetic Psychology 109, 205-229.

Di Vesta, F. J. and Dick, W. (1966) The test-retest reliability of children's ratings on the semantic differential. Educational and Psychological Measurement 26, 605-616.

Dunphy, T. and MacKinnon, N. J. (2002) A Proposal for Integrating Folklore and Affect Control Theory. Electronic Journal of Sociology 6, 3.

Ekman, P. (2004) *Emotions Revealed: Recognizing Faces and Feelings to Improve Communication and Emotional Life*. Henry Holt & Company, New York.

Elliott, L. L. and Tannenbaum, P. H. (1963) Factor structure of semantic differential responses to visual forms and prediction of factor-scores from structural characteristics of the stimulus-shapes. American Journal of Psychology 76, 589-597.

Fararo, T. J. (1989) *The Meaning of General Theoretical Sociology: Tradition and Formalization*. Cambridge University Press, New York.

Fillmore, C. (1968) The case for case. In: E. Bach and R. Harms (Eds.), *Universals of Linguistic Theory*. Holt, Rinehart and Winston, New York.

Fontenelle, T. (2003) FrameNet and Frame Semantics. A Special Issue of International Journal of Lexicography. Vol. 16 (Number 3).

Francis, C. A. (2006) Affect control theory: An introduction. In: K. McClelland and T. J. Fararo (Eds.), *Purpose, Meaning, and Action: Control Systems Theories in Sociology*. Palgrave Macmillan, New York, pp. 139-161.

Francis, C. A. and Heise, D. R. (2006) Emotions on the job: Supporting and threatening face in work organizations. 2006 Social Structure and Emotion Conference, Department of Sociology, University of Georgia, Athens, GA.

Francis, L. E. (1997a) Emotion, coping, and therapeutic ideologies. Social Perspectives on Emotion 4, 71-101.

Francis, L. E. (1997b) Ideology and interpersonal emotion management: Redefining identity in two support groups. Social Psychology Quarterly 60, 153-171.

Friedkin, N. E. (1998) *A Structural Theory of Social Influence*. Cambridge University Press, New York.

Friedkin, N. E. and Johnsen, E. C. (2003) Attitude change, affect control, and expectations states in the formation of influence networks. Advances in Group Processes 20, 1-29.

Goffman, E. (1959) *Presentation of Self in Everyday Life*. Anchor, Garden City, NY.

Goffman, E. (1961) *Asylums*. Doubleday, Garden City, NY.

Goffman, E. (1963) *Stigma: Notes on the Management of Spoiled Identity*. Simon & Schuster (Touchstone), New York.

Goffman, E. (1967) *Interaction Ritual: Essays on Face-to-Face Behavior*. Anchor Books, Garden City, NY.

Gollob, H. F. (1968) Impression formation and word combination in sentences. Journal of Personality and Social Psychology 10, 341-53.

Gollob, H. F. (1974) A subject-verb-object approach to social cognition. Psychological Review 81, 286-321.

Gollob, H. F. and Rossman, B. B. (1973) Judgments of an actor's 'Power and ability to influence others'. Journal of Experimental Social Psychology 9, 391-406.

Gordon, R. A., Short, J. F. J., Cartwright, D. S. and Strodtbeck, F. L. (1963) Values and gang delinquency: A study of street corner groups. American Journal of Sociology 69, 109-128.

Heise, D. R. (1965) Semantic Differential Profiles for 1,000 Most Frequent English Words. Psychological Monographs 79, Whole Issue No. 601.

Heise, D. R. (1966a) Sensitization of verbal response-dispositions by n Affiliation and n Achievement. Journal of Verbal Learning and Verbal Behavior 5, 522-25.

Heise, D. R. (1966b) Social status, attitudes, and word connotations. Sociological Inquiry 36, 227-39.

Heise, D. R. (1966c) Sound-meaning correlations among 1,000 English words. Language and Speech 9, 14-27.

Heise, D. R. (1967) Prefatory findings in the sociology of missions. Journal for the Scientific Study of Religion 6, 49-58.

Heise, D. R. (1969a) Affective dynamics in simple sentences. Journal of Personality and Social Psychology 11, 204-13.

Heise, D. R. (1969b) Some methodological issues in semantic differential research. Psychological Bulletin 72, 406-422.

Heise, D. R. (1970a) Potency dynamics in simple sentences. Journal of Personality and Social Psychology 16, 48-54.

Heise, D. R. (1970b) The semantic differential and attitude research. In: G. Summers (Ed.), *Attitude Measurement*. Rand McNally, Chicago, pp. 235-53.

Heise, D. R. (1977) Social action as the control of affect. Behavioral Science 22, 163-177.

Heise, D. R. (1978) *Computer-Assisted Analysis of Social Action: Use of Program INTERACT and SURVEY.UNC75*. Institute for Research in the Social Sciences, Chapel Hill, NC.

Heise, D. R. (1979) *Understanding Events: Affect and the Construction of Social Action*. Cambridge University Press, New York.

Heise, D. R. (1982a) Face synthesizer. Micro: The 6502/6809 Journal 49, 31-37.

Heise, D. R. (1982b) Measuring attitudes with a PET. BYTE: The Small Systems Journal 7, 208-246.

Heise, D. R. (1985a) Affect control theory: Respecification, estimation, and tests of the formal model. Journal of Mathematical Sociology 11, 191-222.

Heise, D. R. (1985b) Facial expression of emotion as a means of socialization. Electronic Social Psychology 1.

Heise, D. R. (1986) Modeling symbolic interaction. In: J. S. Coleman and S. Nowak (Eds.), *Approaches to Social Theory*. Russell Sage Foundation, New York, pp. 291-309.

Heise, D. R. (1987a) Affect control theory: Concepts and model. Journal of Mathematical Sociology 13, 1-33.

Heise, D. R. (1987b) Sociocultural determination of mental aging. In: C. Schooler and K. W. Schaie (Eds.), *Cognitive Functioning and Social Structure Over the Life Course*. Ablex, Norwood, NJ, pp. 247-261.

Heise, D. R. (1989) Effects of emotion displays on social identification. Social Psychology Quarterly 52, 10-21.

Heise, D. R. (1990a) Affect control model technical appendix. In: T. D. Kemper (Ed.), *Research Agendas in the Sociology of Emotions*. State University of New York Press, Albany, NY, pp. 271-280.

Heise, D. R. (1990b) Careers, career trajectories, and the self. In: J. Rodin, C. Schooler and K. W. Schaie (Eds.), *Self-Directedness: Cause and Effects Throughout the Life Course*. Lawrence Erlbaum Associates, New York, pp. 59-84.

Heise, D. R. (1997) Interact On-Line (Java applet). Last accessed July 1, 2006; www.indiana.edu/~socpsy/ACT/interact/JavaInteract.html.

Heise, D. R. (1998) Conditions for Empathic Solidarity. In: P. Doreian and T. J. Fararo (Eds.), *The Problem of Solidarity: Theories and Models*. Gordon and Breach, Amsterdam, pp. 197-211.

Heise, D. R. (1999) Controlling Affective Experience Interpersonally. Social Psychology Quarterly 62 4-16.

Heise, D. R. (2000a) Affect control theory and impression formation. In: E. F. Borgatta and R. J. Montgomery (Eds.), *Encyclopedia of Sociology*. Macmillan Reference, New York, pp. 41-47.

Heise, D. R. (2000b) Thinking sociologically with mathematics. Sociological Theory 18, 498-504.

Heise, D. R. (2001) Project Magellan: Collecting Cross-Cultural Affective Meanings Via the Internet. Electronic Journal of Sociology 5.

Heise, D. R. (2002) Understanding Social Interaction with Affect Control Theory. In: J. Berger and M. J. Zelditch (Eds.), *New Directions in Contemporary Sociological Theory.* Rowman & Littlefield, New York, pp. 17-40.

Heise, D. R. (2004) Enculturating agents with expressive role behavior. In: S. Payer and R. Trappl (Eds.), *Agent Culture: Human-Agent Interaction in a Multicultural World.* Lawrence Erlbaum, Mahwah, NJ, pp. 127-142.

Heise, D. R. (2005) Magellan.Surveyor Documentation. Indiana University, last accessed July 2, 2006; http://www.indiana.edu/~socpsy/ACT/SurveyorDocumentation.htm.

Heise, D. R. (2006) Sentiment formation in social interaction. In: K. McClelland and T. J. Fararo (Eds.), *Purpose, Meaning, and Action : Control Systems Theories in Sociology.* Palgrave Macmillan, New York, pp. 189-211.

Heise, D. R. and Calhan, C. (1995) Emotion norms in interpersonal events. Social Psychology Quarterly 58, 223-240.

Heise, D. R. and Durig, A. (1997) A Frame for Organizational Actions and Macroactions. Journal of Mathematical Sociology 22, 95-123.

Heise, D. R. and Lerner, S. J. (2006) Affect control in international interactions. Social Forces.

Heise, D. R. and Lewis, E. (1988) Programs Interact and Attitude: Software and Documentation. Wm. C. Brown Publishers, Dubuque, IA.

Heise, D. R. and MacKinnon, N. J. (1987) Affective bases of likelihood perception. Journal of Mathematical Sociology 13, 133-151.

Heise, D. R. and O'Brien, J. (1993) Emotion expression in groups. In: M. Lewis and J. M. Haviland (Eds.), *The Handbook of Emotions.* Guilford Press, New York, pp. 489-497.

Heise, D. R. and Smith-Lovin, L. (1981) Impressions of goodness, powerfulness and liveliness from discerned social events. Social Psychology Quarterly 44, 93-106.

Heise, D. R. and Thomas, L. (1989) Predicting impressions created by combinations of emotion and social identity. Social Psychology Quarterly 52, 141-148.

Heise, D. R. and Weir, B. (1999) A test of symbolic interactionist predictions about emotions in imagined situations. Symbolic Interaction 22 129-161.

Hochschild, A. (1983) *The Managed Heart: Commercialization of Human Feeling.* University of California Press, Berkeley.

Holmes, T. and David, E. (1989) *Life Change, Life Events, and Illness.* Praeger, New York.

Holstein, J. A. and Gubrium, J. J. (2000) *The Self We Live By: Narrative Identity in a Postmodern World.* Oxford University Press, New York.

Irwin, K. (2003) Political Interaction and Affective Meaning. M.A. Thesis, Department of Sociology, University of Missouri, St. Louis.

Jenkins, J. J., Russell, W. A. and Suci, G. C. (1958) An atlas of semantic profiles for 360 words. American Journal of Psychology 71, 688-699.

Jonas, L. (1999) Making and facing danger: Constructing strong character on the river. Symbolic Interaction 23, 247-67.

Kalkhoff, W. (2002) Delinquency and violence as affect-control: Reviving the subcultural approach in criminology. Electronic Journal of Sociology 6, 3.

Kemper, T. D. (1978) *A Social Interactional Theory of Emotion.* Wiley, New York.

Kemper, T. D. (1991) An introduction to the sociology of emotions. International Review of Studies on Emotion 1, 301-349.

Kemper, T. D. and Collins, R. (1990) Dimensions of microinteraction. American Journal of Sociology 96, 32-68.

Kim, J. (2004) Dimensionality of Affective Meaning and Social Identities in China and Korea. Last accessed June 1, 2006; http://www.indiana.edu/~socpsy/ACT/Seminar2/Seminar_2.htm.

King, A. B. (2001) Affective dimensions of internet culture. Social Science Computer Review 19, 414-430.

Kirby, D. M. and Gardner, R. C. (1972) Ethnic stereotypes: Norms on 208 words typically used in their assessment. Canadian Journal of Psychology 26, 140-154.

Kroska, A. (1997) The division of labor in the home: A review and reconceptualization. Social Psychology Quarterly 60, 304-322.

Kroska, A. (2001) Do we have consensus? Examining the relationship between gender ideology and role meanings. Social Psychology Quarterly 64, 18-40.

Langford, T. and MacKinnon, N. J. (2000) The affective basis for the gendering of traits: Comparing the United States and Canada. Social Psychology Quarterly 63, 34-48.

Lawson, E. D. (1973) Men's first names, nicknames, and short names: A semantic differential analysis. Names 21, 22-27.

Lawson, E. D. and Roeder, L. M. (1986) Women's full names, short names and affectionate names: A semantic differential analysis. Names 34, 175-84.

Lee, B. and Shafer, C. S. (2002) The dynamic nature of leisure experience: An application of affect control theory. Journal of Leisure Research 34, 290-310.

Lerner, S. J. (1983) Affective Dynamics of International Relations. Ph.D. Dissertation, Department of Sociology, University of North Carolina, Chapel Hill, NC.

Liedka, R. V. (1995) Status, power and expressivity as the basis of occupational grading: Multidimensional analyses. Department of Sociology. Cornell University, Ithaca, NY.

Lively, K. J. and Heise, D. R. (2004) Sociological realms of emotional experience. American Journal of Sociology 109, 1109-36.

Lively, K. J. and Powell, B. (2006) Emotional expression at work and at home: Domain, status, or individual characteristics. Social Psychology Quarterly 69, 17-38.

Lovaglia, M., Youngreen, R. and Robinson, D. T. (2005) Identity maintenance, affect control, and cognitive performance. Advances in Group Processes 22, 65-92.

MacKinnon, N. J. (1985/1988/1998) Final Reports to Social Sciences and Humanities Research Council of Canada on Projects 410-81-0089, 410-86-0794, and 410-94-0087. Department of Sociology and Anthropology, University of Guelph, Ontario, Canada.

MacKinnon, N. J. (1994) Symbolic Interactionism as Affect Control. State University of New York Press, Albany, NY.

MacKinnon, N. J. (2003) Symbolic interaction and knowledge presentation: From cognitive to affective models. Keynote address at Conference on Preparing for the Future of Knowledge Presentation. International Institute for Information Design, Institute of Design, Illinois Institute of Technology, Chicago, IL.

MacKinnon, N. J. and Bowlby, J. W. (2000) The Affective Dynamics of Stereotyping and Intergroup Relations. Advances in Group Processes 17, 37-76.

MacKinnon, N. J. and Heise, D. R. (1993) Affect control theory: Delineation and development. In: J. Berger and M. J. Zelditch (Eds.), Theoretical Research Programs: Studies in the Growth of Theory. Stanford University Press, Stanford, CA.

MacKinnon, N. J. and Goulbourne, M. M. (2006) The affect control theory of emotions: The case of depression. In: K. McClelland and T. J. Fararo (Eds.), Purpose, Meaning, and Action: Control Sytems Theories in Sociology. Palgrave Macmillan, New York, pp. 237-266.

MacKinnon, N. J. and Heise, D. R. (2006) Identities, Selves, and Social Institutions. Department of Sociology, Indiana University.

MacKinnon, N. J. and Keating, L. (1989) The structure of emotion: A review of the problem and a cross-cultural analysis. Social Psychology Quarterly 52, 70-83.

MacKinnon, N. J. and Langford, T. (1994) The meaning of occupational prestige scores: A social psychological analysis and interpretation. Sociological Quarterly 35, 215-245.

MacKinnon, N. J. and Luke, A. (2002) Changes in identity attitudes as reflections of social and cultural change. Canadian Journal of Sociology 27, 299-338.

Malone, M. J. (2004) Structure and affect: The influence of social structure on affective meaning in American kinship. Social Psychology Quarterly 67, 203-216.

Maltz, H. E. (1963) Ontogenetic change in the meaning of concepts as measured by the semantic differential. Child Development 34, 667-674.

Marks, I. M. (1965) *Patterns of Meaning in Psychiatric Patients: Semantic Differential Responses in Obsessives and Psychopaths.* Oxford University Press, London.

Marks, I. M. (1966) Semantic differential uses in psychiatric patients: A study of obsessive, psychopath, and control inpatients. British Journal of Psychiatry 112, 945-951.

McCall, G. J. and Simmons, J. L. (1978) *Identities and Interactions.* 2nd edition, Free Press, New York.

McClelland, K. and Fararo, T. J. (Eds.) (2006) *Purpose, Meaning, and Action: Control Systems Theories in Sociology.* Palgrave Macmillan, New York.

Miller, G. A. (1991) *The Science of Words.* Scientific American Library, New York.

Moore, C. D. and Robinson, D. T. (2006) Selective identity preferences: Choosing form among alternative occupational identities. Advances in Group Processes 23, 253-281.

Morgan, R. and Heise, D. R. (1988) Structure of Emotions. Social Psychology Quarterly 51, 19-31.

Ortony, A., Clore, G. L. and Foss, M. (1987) The referential structure of the affective lexicon. Cognitive Science 11, 341-364.

Osgood, C. E. (1962) Studies of the generality of affective meaning systems. American Psychologist 17, 10-28.

Osgood, C. E. (1966) Dimensionality of the semantic space for communication via facial expressions. Scandanavian Journal of Psychology 7, 1-30.

Osgood, C. E. (1969) On the whys and wherefores of EPA. Journal of Personality and Social Psychology 12, 194-199.

Osgood, C. E., May, W. H. and Miron, M. S. (1975) *Cross-Cultural Universals of Affective Meaning.* University of Illinois Press, Urbana.

Osgood, C. E., Suci, G. C. and Tannenbaum, P. H. (1957) *The Measurement of Meaning.* University of Illinois Press, Urbana.

Pavloski, R. (1989) The physiological stress of thwarted intentions. In: W. A. Hershberger (Ed.), *Volitional Action.* Elsvier Science Publishers, Amsterdam.

Piaget, J. (1954) *The Construction of Reality in the Child.* Basic Books, New York.

Powers, W. T. (1973) *Behavior: The Control of Perception.* Aldine, Chicago.

Rashotte, L. S. (2001) Some effects of demeanor on the meaning of behaviors in context. Current Research in Social Psychology 6, 17.

Rashotte, L. S. (2002a) Incorporating nonverbal behaviors into affect control theory. Electronic Journal of Sociology 6, 3.

Rashotte, L. S. (2002b) What does that smile mean? The meaning of nonverbal behaviors in social interaction. Social Psychology Quarterly 65, 92-102.

Rashotte, L. S. (2003) Written versus visual stimuli in the study of impression formation. Social Science Research 32, 278-293.

Raynolds, P. A., Sakamoto, S. and Raynolds, G. H. (1988) Consistent projective differential responses by American and Japanese students. Perceptual and Motor Skills 66, 395-402.

Raynolds, P. A., Sakamoto, S. and Saxe, R. (1981) Consistent responses by groups of subjects to projective differential items. Perceptual and Motor Skills 53, 635-644.

Ridgeway, C. and Smith-Lovin, L. (1994) Structure, culture, and interaction: Comparing two generative theories. Advances in Group Processes 11, 213-239.

Robins, L. N. (1966) *Deviant Children Grown Up: A Sociological and Psychiatric Study of Sociopathic Personality.* Williams & Wilkins, Baltimore.

Robins, R. W., Trzesniewski, K. H., Tracy, J. L., Gosling, S. D. and Potter, J. (2002) Global self-esteem across the life span. Psychology and Aging 17, 423-34.

Robinson, D. T. (1996) Identity and friendship: Affective dynamics and network formation. Advances in Group Processes 13, 91-111.

Robinson, D. T., Rogalin, C. L. and Smith-Lovin, L. (2004) Physiological measures of theoretical concepts: Some ideas for linking deflection and emotion to physical responses during interaction. Advances in Group Processes 21, 77-115.

Robinson, D. T. and Smith-Lovin, L. (1992) Selective interaction as a strategy for identity maintenance: An affect control model. Social Psychology Quarterly 55, 12-28.

Robinson, D. T. and Smith-Lovin, L. (1999) Emotion display as a strategy for identity negotiation. Motivation and Emotion 23, 73-104.

Robinson, D. T. and Smith-Lovin, L. (2006) Affect Control Theory. In: P. Burke (Ed.), *Contemporary Social Psychological Theories*. Stanford University Press, Stanford, CA, pp. 137-164.

Robinson, D. T., Smith-Lovin, L. and Tsoudis, O. (1994) Heinous crime or unfortunate accident? The effects of remorse on responses to mock criminal confessions. Social Forces 73, 175-190.

Rogers, C. R. (1961) *On Becoming a Person; A Therapist's View of Psychotherapy.* Houghton Mifflin, Boston.

Romney, A. K., Batchelder, W. H. and Weller, S. C. (1987) Recent applications of cultural consensus theory. American Behavioral Science 31, 163-177.

Romney, A. K., Weller, S. C. and Batchelder, W. H. (1986) Culture as consensus: A theory of culture and informant accuracy. American Anthropologist 88, 313-338.

Schafer, R. B. and Keith, P. M. (1999) Change in adult self-esteem: A longitudinal assessment. British Journal of Social Psychology 38, 303-314.

Scher, S. J. and Heise, D. R. (1993) Affect and the perception of injustice. Advances in Group Processes 10 223-252.

Schneider, A. (1996) Sexual-erotic emotions in the U.S. in cross-cultural comparison. International Journal of Sociology and Social Policy 16, 123-143.

Schneider, A. (1999a) Emergent clusters of denotative meaning. Electronic Journal of Sociology 4, 2.

Schneider, A. (1999b) The violent character of sexual-eroticism in cross-cultural comparison. International Journal of Sociology and Social Policy 18, 81-100.

Schneider, A. (1999c) U.S. Neo-Conservatism: Cohort and Cross-Cultural Perspective. International Journal of Sociology and Social Policy 19, 56-86

Schneider, A. (2002a) Computer simulation of behavior prescriptions in multi-cultural corporations. Organization Studies 23, 105-131.

Schneider, A. (2002b) Probing Unknown Cultures. Electronic Journal of Sociology 6, 3.

Schneider, A. and Heise, D. R. (1995) Simulating Symbolic Interaction. Journal of Mathematical Sociology 20, 271-287.

Smith, H. W. (1995) Predicting stress in American-Japanese business relations. Journal of Asian Business 12, 79-89.

Smith, H. W. (2002) The dynamics of Japanese and American interpersonal events: Behavioral settings versus personality traits. Journal of Mathematical Sociology 26, 1-21.

Smith, H. W. and Francis, L. E. (2005) Social versus self-directed events among Japanese and Americans: Self-actualization, emotions, moods, and trait disposition labeling. Social Forces 84, 821-830.

Smith, H. W., Ike, S. and Yeng, L. (2002) Project Magellan redux: Problems and solutions with collecting cross-cultural affective meanings via the Internet. Electronic Journal of Sociology 6, 3.

Smith, H. W., Matsuno, T. and Ike, S. (2001) The affective basis of attributional processes among Japanese and Americans. Social Psychology Quarterly 64, 180-194.

Smith, H. W., Matsuno, T. and Umino, M. (1994) How similar are impression-formation processes among Japanese and Americans? Social Psychology Quarterly 57, 124-139.

Smith, H. W., Umino, M. and Matsuno, T. (1998) The formation of gender-differentiated sentiments in Japan. Journal of Mathematical Sociology 22, 373-395.

Smith, H. W. and Yap, M. (2006) Guilty Americans and shameful Japanese? An affect control test of Benedict's thesis. In: K. McClelland and T. J. Fararo (Eds.), *Purpose, Meaning and Action: Control Systems Theories in Sociology*. Palgrave Macmillan, New York, pp. 213-236.

Smith-Lovin, L. (1979) Behavior settings and impressions formed from social scenarios. Social Psychology Quarterly 42, 31-43.

Smith-Lovin, L. (1987a) Affect control theory: An assessment. Journal of Mathematical Sociology 13, 171-192.

Smith-Lovin, L. (1987b) Impressions from events. Journal of Mathematical Sociology 13, 35-70.

Smith-Lovin, L. (1987c) The affective control of events within settings. Journal of Mathematical Sociology 13, 71-101.

Smith-Lovin, L. (1990) Emotion as the confirmation and disconfirmation of identity: An affect control model. In: T. D. Kemper (Ed.), *Research Agendas in the Sociology of Emotions*. State University of New York Press, Albany, NY, pp. 238-270.

Smith-Lovin, L. (1991) An affect control view of cognition and emotion. In: J. A. Howard and P. L. Callero (Eds.), *The Self-Society Dynamic: Cognition, Emotion, and Action*. Cambridge University Press, New York, pp. 143-169.

Smith-Lovin, L. (1993) Can emotionality and rationality be reconciled? A comment on Collins, Frank, Hirshleifer, and Jasso. Rationality and Society 5, 283-293.

Smith-Lovin, L. (2002) Roles, identities, and emotions: Parallel processing and the production of mixed emotions. In: Y. Kashima, M. Foddy and M. J. Platow (Eds.), *Self and Identity: Personal, Social, and Symbolic*. Lawrence Erlbaum Associates, Mahwah NJ, pp. 125-143.

Smith-Lovin, L. (2003) Self, identity, and interaction in an ecology of identities. In: P. J. Burke, T. J. Owens, P. A. Thoits and R. T. Serpe (Eds.), *Advances in Identity Theory and Research*. Plenum, New York, pp. 167-178.

Smith-Lovin, L. and Douglass, W. (1992) An affect-control analysis of two religious groups. Social Perspectives on Emotion 1, 217-247.

Smith-Lovin, L. and Heise, D. R. (1982) A structural equation model of impression formation. In: N. Hirschberg and L. G. Humphreys (Eds.), *Multivariate Applications in the Social Sciences*. Lawrence Erlbaum, Hillsdale, NJ, pp. 195-222.

Smith-Lovin, L. and Heise, D. R. (Eds.) (1988) *Analyzing Social Interaction: Advances in Affect Control Theory*. Gordon and Breach, New York.

Smith-Lovin, L. and Robinson, D. T. (1992) Gender and conversational dynamics. In: C. Ridgeway (Ed.), *Gender, Interaction and Inequality*. Springer-Verlag, New York, pp. 122-156.

Smith-Lovin, L. and Robinson, D. T. (2006) Control theories of identity, action, and emotion: In search of testable differences between affect control theory and identity control theory. In: K. McClelland and T. J. Fararo (Eds.), *Purpose, Meaning, and Action : Control Systems Theories in Sociology*. Palgrave MacMillan, New York, pp. 163-188.

Smith-Lovin, L., Robinson, D. T. and Wisecup, A. (2006) Affect control theory and emotions. In: J. E. Stets and J. Turner (Eds.), *Handbook of the Sociology of Emotions*. Springer, New York.

Snider, J. G. and Osgood, C. E. (1969) *Semantic Differential Technique: A Sourcebook*. Aldine, Chicago.

Solley, C. M. and Messick, S. J. (1957) Probability, learning, the statistical structure of concepts, and the measurement of meaning. American Journal of Psychology 70, 161-73.

Thoits, P. A. (1994) Stressors and problem-solving: The individual as psychological activist. Journal of Health and Social Behavior 35, 143-59.

Thomas, L. and Heise, D. R. (1995) Mining error variance and hitting pay-dirt: Discovering systematic variation in social sentiments. Sociological Quarterly 36, Number , pages . 425-439.

Thomassen, L. (2002) An alcoholic is good and sober: Sentiment change in AA. Deviant Behavior: An Interdisciplinary Journal 23, 177-200.

Troyer, L. (2004) Affect control theory as a foundation for the design of socially intelligent systems. In *Proceedings of 2004 American Association for Artificial Intelligence Symposium on Architectures for Modeling Emotion: Cross Disciplinary Foundations.* AAAI Press, Menlo Park, CA, pp. 27-30.

Troyer, L. and Robinson, D. T. (2006) Contributions of a microsociological perspective on emotion to the study of political identity and action. In: D. Redlawsk (Ed.), *Feeling Politics: Emotion in Political Information Processing.* Palgrave Macmillan, New York, pp. 47-56.

Tsoudis, O. (2000a) Relation of affect control theory to the sentencing of criminals. Journal of Social Psychology 140, 473-485.

Tsoudis, O. (2000b) The likelihood of victim restitution in mock cases: Are the 'rules of the game' different from prison and probation? Social Behavior and Personality 28, 483-500.

Tsoudis, O. and Smith-Lovin, L. (1998) How bad was it? The effects of victim and perpetrator emotion on responses to criminal court vignettes. Social Forces 77, 695-722.

Tsoudis, O. and Smith-Lovin, L. (2001) Criminal identity: The key to situational construals in mock criminal court cases. Sociological Spectrum 21, 3-31.

Tzeng, O. C. (Ed.) (1990) *Language, Meaning, and Culture: The Selected Papers of C. E. Osgood.* Praeger New York.

Walkey, F. H. and Boshier, R. (1969) Changes in semantic differential responses over two years. Psychological Reports 24, 1008-1010.

Wang, J. (2006) Dimensions In Social Space: A Comparative Study of China, Korea, and America. Department of Sociology, University of Iowa, Iowa City, Iowa.

Wiggins, B. B. and Heise, D. R. (1987) Expectations, intentions, and behavior: Some tests of affect control theory. Journal of Mathematical Sociology 13, 153-169.

Index

status, 22, 23, 27, 34, 52, 76, 101, 136, 142, 145, 147
stereotypes, 23
stress, 47, 56, 60, 61, 62, 63, 75, 137, 147
structure, 17, 47, 57, 59, 60, 62, 63, 107, 109, 114, 131, 132, 134, 135, 136, 137, 146
sub-cultures, 21, 22, 23, 24, 25, 26, 55, 130, 135, 136, 137, 140, 147
supernatural, 29, 61, 67
surveys, 15, 24, 42, 56, 132, 135
Thomassen, Lisa Thomas, 3, 56, 63, 98, 100, 133, 134, 137
traits, 23, 26, 33, 34, 41, 65, 66, 68, 69, 70, 101, 120, 131, 136, 141, 142, 145, 147
transients, 38, 70, 81, 82, 83, 84, 85, 88, 91, 92, 97, 98, 99, 100, 101, 103, 106,

113, 115, 116, 117, 120, 123, 125, 135, 141, 145, 146, 147
trans-situational, 69, 101
Tsoudis, Olga, 72, 135, 137
turn-taking, 47
U.S.A., 3, 7, 10, 11, 17, 18, 19, 22, 23, 24, 44, 56, 131, 137, 143
Umino, Michio, 42, 84, 131, 134, 136
universals, 11, 146
verbs, 35, 36, 42, 43, 143, 146
victimization, 3, 54, 55, 67, 73, 76, 143
weights, 82, 83, 88, 111
work, 3, 4, 11, 26, 27, 28, 29, 30, 32, 34, 36, 37, 42, 43, 44, 45, 47, 48, 50, 51, 52, 54, 56, 57, 63, 66, 67, 69, 70, 71, 72, 73, 74, 76, 77, 119, 123, 129, 130, 131, 132, 133, 134, 135, 136, 137, 139, 143, 145

Printed in the USA